UPON WAKING

JACKIE HILL PERRY

UPON WAKING

B&H
PUBLISHING
BRENTWOOD, TENNESSEE

978-1-0877-8371-0

Published by B&H Publishing Group
Brentwood, Tennessee

Dewey Decimal Classification: 242.5
Subject Heading: DEVOTIONAL LITERATURE
/ CHRISTIAN LIFE / MEDITATIONS

Cover design by B&H Publishing Group. Cover images
by SanderMeertinsPhotography/Shutterstock; Artem
Zarubin/Shutterstock; ilolab/Shutterstock

5 6 7 8 9 10 11 12 • 28 27 26 25 24 23

TO EVERY SAINT THAT TAUGHT ME TO
GIVE GOD MY FIRST HELLO.

ACKNOWLEDGMENTS

Team Wartrace

The saints at B&H

Austin and nem

1. The sum of true wisdom—viz. the knowledge of God and of ourselves. Effects of the latter.

2. Effects of the knowledge of God, in humbling our pride, unveiling our hypocrisy, demonstrating the absolute perfections of God, and our own utter helplessness.

—

Who, in fact, does not thus rest, so long as he is unknown to himself; that is, so long as he is contented with his own endowments, and unconscious or unmindful of his misery? Every person, therefore, on coming to the knowledge of himself, is not only urged to seek God, but is also led as by the hand to find him.

So long as we do not look beyond the earth, we are quite pleased with our own righteousness, wisdom, and virtue; we address ourselves in the most flattering terms, and seem only less than demigods. But should we once begin to raise our thoughts to God, and reflect what kind of Being he is, and how absolute the perfection of that righteousness, and wisdom, and virtue, to which, as a standard, we are bound to be conformed, what formerly delighted us by its false show of righteousness will become polluted with the greatest iniquity.

—John Calvin, *Institutes of the Christian Religion: Book 1*, chapter 1

INTRODUCTION

DEVOTIONALS HAVE NEVER BEEN my cup of tea. A strange way to introduce this book, I know. Seeing that in your hand is, in fact, a devotional. When there is contempt for anything, the process of seeing the good in it usually means adding to it whatever you think is missing. For me, what's missing is depth. Not in all devotional content but in many. The small book, able to fit in one hand or displayed as an ornament on the coffee table, is opened. Day one or thirty is listed at the top of the page. A short Scripture is listed underneath. Followed by a paragraph or two of sentences that are supposed to lift the reader toward God.

All of that is wonderful, but what happens when the words themselves center self and not Jesus? When the sentences are a garden with an inch of dirt, what kind of flowers do we expect to grow from such shallow soil? I recall the works of Oswald Chambers, Charles Spurgeon, and *The Valley of Vision* from which contemporary writers have departed. It is possible to communicate glory in a few words. Because of this, it is my opinion that even the word count restrictions in a devotional format aren't to blame for the lack of depth. It's us. "We are far too easily pleased," as C. S. Lewis said.[1] We can read six sentences, chew the crackers, sip the cup, swallow the piece, and believe ourselves to be full. But surely, if God is the Bread of Life, there is always more.

With that said, this work isn't the meal; it's the appetizer. My attempt to take us beyond the quick and easy is by centering the Scriptures and not the self on each page. Each devotional is exegetically focused or observational in its approach. With either form, the goal is to stir you up. To whet your appetite, if you will, for God and His Word. Each devotional is a shovel. Once the cover is closed, it's your turn to dig. To open the Scriptures, using my observations of them as a resource, not a conclusion. My heart for you is that by seeing Him, then and only then will you discover yourself. Primarily, that you need Him. It's the insufficiency of everything, including devotionals, that signals our need for more than what we've been satisfied with.

What is typical of devotional-like content, we engage only as a means to check off a box or temper our spiritual insecurities. This work cannot become the measure of your maturity in which you read only to feel good enough. Or study only to prove your godliness. You are capable of so much more, and you know it. God made you and redeemed you so that you may know Him. That's the point of everything. And that's the point of this book. To cultivate in you the desire for God. I can promise you that a sixty-day devotional cannot do that for you. God sent Christ to die for sin, overcoming the penalty and power of it so that you can know Him. And Christ sent the Spirit to fill the saints so that you can know Him. He is the sufficient one. So if ever you finish a page on day one or sixty and notice that you're still hungry, good! Your stomach is being made ready for more. Be reminded that the bread isn't in this book. It's in the One this book is pointing toward. Close the page, return the book to its place because dinner is ready. The Scriptures are the meal and Christ is its bread. Go to Him and be filled.

And when He had given thanks, He broke [the
bread] and said, "Take, eat; this is My body which
is broken for you." 1 CORINTHIANS 11:24 NKJV

BEFORE WORK OR WHATEVER it is that obligates our time
after waking, we eat, even if we ate six to nine hours before.
Before bed we eat to cease the hunger. After the risen sun
and early yawn, we do the same. This is science. Biological.
Human. Fuel is a perpetual need to which our bodies would
break if kept from it. On those spiritual days when we fast,
withholding food from the body, we taste what starvation
does to us. The mind twists and turns. Our emotions sway
and, if turned in the wrong direction, tempt us to burn
everything to the ground. Monday through Sunday we are
largely controlled by our stomachs and if anything is in it. So
much so that its contents determine if we will be a Monster
or a Mercy.

I don't find it odd, then, that our Lord uses food as a metaphor for Himself. The most memorable being that of bread.
The whole subject began when Jesus told Israel the Father
has bread to give them that is true (John 6:32). Figuring that
Jesus's preaching about bread must mean He had access to a

better manna, they heard this and contemplated a different miracle. One of constant sustenance. "Sir, give us this bread always," they said (John 6:34). Always. They supposed Jesus was offering to fill their belly and not their soul. With a product made of wheat, planted in the soil, grown from the ground, harvested by human hands. That might've been bread, but that bread was not the better manna. The true bread was and is Jesus, He who said, "I am the bread of life" and "I am the living bread that came down from heaven" (John 6:35, 51).

You may be wondering where I am going by saying all of this. Wondering how my original point connects to my most recent, and it is this: in the same way our bodies need a constant diet of food, our souls need God like this always. Upon waking, we are hungry for heaven, and yet we fill it with a scroll or many. As the day moves forward and the belly still empty, we fill it again, when a person gives us a measure of love, a like, a look. Before bed, the soul, if visible, would be skeletal. Barely able to stand on its own or smile with all of its teeth. The body who holds this almost-dead thing feels alive because it depends on every other bread except the One the Father sent.

But the Lord's Table has been set, so sit. Revive yourself in His life. Fill yourself in His love. Scrape the plate and wipe it clean. We need the Bread of heaven because truly no other food will do.

Devote yourselves to prayer with an alert mind
and a thankful heart. COLOSSIANS 4:2 NLT

NO ONE LIKES TO be bored. Especially now, in this age, with a million ways to be entertained. Things like the optionality of commercials reinforces our impatience. When only a decade or so ago, sitting through an advertisement with twiddling thumbs was an obligation. Now it's a choice no one makes. Keep the entertainment going we say.

Then there's the wonderfully terrible invention of social media that entertains without ceasing. Like the Colosseum in our hands. In one swipe, videos of a recipe, a twelve-second sermon, a slam dunk, a knee on a neck, an article about nothing or everything, a riot at the Capitol and a dog singing Sinatra.

It's no wonder that when it's time to pray, the length and consistency of the prayer suffers under the weight of a mind that's completely uncomfortable with boredom. In whatever quiet place you've chosen, in your car or in your closet, you sit or lie, kneel or stand. Closing your eyes, you begin, as usual, "Our Father" or something like it. Then you remember you forgot to get some paper towels for the kitchen. "Who art in heaven . . ." Then there's the online meeting you have on Thursday. "Hallowed be Your name." And why didn't Daddy buy the bike you asked for when you were twelve? At this point, you have two options: keep sitting with God in the silence of everything, or give into the noise in your mind, which, if you're honest, feels more entertaining than intimacy.

"Think of boredom during silent prayer as an act of purification," one pastor recommends. "In this uneventful moment, God purifies us of the false god of good feelings. Silent prayer is often something I want to avoid because it forces me to exorcise the demons of excitement, stimulation, and distraction."[2] On some level, regaining discipline over your prayer life will happen as you rediscover the beauty of boredom. As long as you need to be doing, writing, reading, laughing at, watching something to have joy, prayer will be of no interest to you. But if you pause and remember the beginning of the prayer again—"Our Father, who art in heaven, hallowed be Your name"—you will remember God, the aim of every prayer. Whether in a closet or a car, the One to whom you speak is holy in heaven, transcendent in nature, yet relational and therefore near to you, His child. He is most interesting. Most intriguing. Not entertaining *per se*, but completely worthy of your mind's focus. And trust me, distractions will happen. It's a part of what it means for you to be you. But every time your mind wanders, just find your way back to God again and again and again.

So I say, "I am grieved
that the right hand of the Most High has changed."
I will remember the Lord's works;
yes, I will remember your ancient wonders.
I will reflect on all you have done
and meditate on your actions. PSALM 77:10-12 CSB

GOD'S WORD AND GOD'S nature must inform your emotions. In saying this, I don't mean feelings are unnecessary when, in fact, emotions are useful for many things. As utilitarian as they might be however, they become a danger to us and the world whenever they are detached from God's Word.

For example, think of the ten spies who looked at the giants in Caanan, felt fear, and forgot God. Or consider David who walked his roof, observing a woman in covenant with another, feeling passion, and forgot purity of heart. Or Peter who inhabited a garden not only with his Lord but also with the men into whose hands his Lord had been delivered, and as his Lord was being taken, Peter felt a lot of things. Maybe fear, maybe zeal. Either way, after a sword was raised, an ear was removed. Feeling what he felt, he forgot the kingdom. When emotions are given underserved supremacy, they can lead us to respond to ourselves, others, and our circumstances in ways that reflect the emotion more than it does their Creator.

At this point, by singling out the negative influence emotions can have, one might see emotions as an enemy of faith. That too would be an irrational, or even emotional, way of seeing things. Emotions are good, for not only did our Lord make them, but He also has them. The issue then is not simply what or how we feel but how what we've inherited from Adam leads us to respond to said feelings.

To say it another way, emotions aren't the problem; the flesh is. So then, in becoming more holy, doing away with emotions won't serve us. What will is that God-breathed Word, both written and living—written in every narrative, epistle, prophet, and psalm, and living in the enfleshed God of heaven. Who, after ascending to that glorious right hand, together with His Father, sent their Spirit who once hovered the waters to not just hover over but fully indwell the people for whom Christ died. These people will feel all kinds of ways all of the time, but they can and they must reflect God's nature when they do.

My God, my God, why have you forsaken me? PSALM 22:1

WHILE READING THE PSALMS, I'm struck by how often God is questioned. Why He's allowing this. Why He's forsaken that. Suffering makes you curious, and to me, it seems, being inquisitive is in fact a healthy part of prayer. Even Jesus, in His dying hour, asked God a question.

I'm not sure who taught us to deny God our questions. If I were to guess, it must've come from the elders of Israel who didn't want us to be irreverent. They knew God was a consuming fire, who descended onto mountains that couldn't be touched. Every generation after them is just as stiff-necked as they were and therefore prone to testing God like their soul wasn't on the line. So I won't deny them the dignity of having good intentions.

But neither should we deny Scripture's testimony regarding this subject. Godly people ask God questions, and why shouldn't they? His ways are not our ways. His thoughts are not our thoughts. The way God moves doesn't often align with our own logic since He doesn't share our nature or essence. We run from pain; He uses it. We hate our enemies;

He loves them. We try to hold onto our life with clinched fists, and He commands another way. The way of death which somehow, someway, causes us to find the life we thought we were losing.

Life with a transcendent God isn't always going to make sense, and if that is the case, questions will be commonplace. When our aversion to prayerful curiosity has lifted, I often wonder if we will discover what we've withheld from God. And by what, I mean our very self. Avoiding curiosity can be a luxury in some sense. To ask anything at all, you have to acknowledge your intellectual limitations. But not only that: to ask anything at all, you have to sit inside whatever tension your body, life, and mind have brought about. Uncovering what hurts, hurts. Thinking about whatever is unclear is frustrating. If you decide not to ask God any questions regarding these things, you can go on with your life, maintain your sense of control and manufactured peace. But to do that is to deny yourself the opportunity of giving God your whole self.

What if asking God questions is one way to cultivate intimacy with God? What if your questions became a door by which you could be vulnerable with Him? What if your questions opened up your mind to read the Scriptures with Spirit-empowered expectation instead of apathetic drudgery? If, in fact, Jesus is the wisdom of God (1 Cor. 1:24), what if, by asking questions, you discover God; and by finding God, you find your answers?

Pray at all times in the Spirit with every prayer and
request, and stay alert with all perseverance and
intercession for all the saints. EPHESIANS 6:18 CSB

I USED TO BELIEVE prayerlessness had everything to do
with time. If I didn't pray, it was because the day got ahead
of me. The clock is a lot like my oldest daughter, an untem-
pered leader. The calendar too. Every single day there is
something to do. Much of which is good. Working from home
or an office. Lunch with friends from school, or church,
or wherever. Then there are the pesky duties like laundry.
Somewhere in the world, there's a pile of clothes on the cold
side of the bed, abandoned and ignored for better joys. When
there are life, friends, church, children, school, husbands,
wives, nine-to-fives and five-to-nines, where in the world is
prayer supposed to fit? This all made sense to me. It gave
me a reason and a finger to point until I opened the Gospels
and saw the truth.

Truth is, Jesus was busy too. The Father had business Jesus
came to handle. A woman at a well to give water to. A
Lazarus to raise. Streets to straighten. Wine to turn. Bodies to
heal. Even at rest, when a few waves prompted the disciples

to wake Him, He got to work by speaking peace. And yet, at no point in any Gospel do you see Him neglect prayer. He made it His business to meet with the Father, sometimes in the morning and other times all the way through the night. Often before making decisions and creating miracles. Even on His dying day, He met with God about a cup, and while it was poured, He spoke with God on a cross (Matt. 26:39; 27:46).

There was no way, in heaven or on earth, that anything would ever keep Jesus from meeting with the Father. Time has never been the reason anyone doesn't pray; the heart is. Prayerlessness is almost always a humility issue—the natural consequence of a heart that tends to believe it is good without God. Yes, you may be busy, but it's possible that you are also proud. Pride is the true enemy of your prayer life. Pride deludes us into thinking we're self-sufficient. That our jobs supply our needs. Our relationships provide comfort. Our intellect and ambition make us successful. But in fact, everything you are and everything you have is because God rains on the just and the unjust (Matt. 5:45).

So then, to become more prayerful, we have to be humble. To be humble, we need to be honest. Each morning, tell the truth. The truth being, you are needy even when it doesn't feel like it. Then, turn toward God and pray.

> Therefore, if anyone is in Christ, he is a new
> creation; the old has passed away, and see,
> the new has come! 2 CORINTHIANS 5:17 CSB

TO BE CALLED A "new creature" is a glorious, praiseworthy attribution. You, if Christ is who you're in, are new. As in, different, novel, recently made. What is typical about you is that you have and will always be a creature. The only One who isn't is God. Everything else is made. A derivative of the eternal One.

The fact you're a creature has never been the problem; the issue has always been your resistance to the submission your creatureliness requires. All things were made through Him and for Him (Col. 1:16). If you were made, then you were made for Someone higher than yourself. The first human creature, Adam, ruined that concept for you. Original sin, as its called, trained you to hate your maker and the limitations of being made. Your entire life, you tried with all of your might to live independent of God. Denying yourself of life with all the breath He gave. You thought the world was yours, your body too. Those delusions were natural to you. Darkness was your native country.

But then, not because of anything you ever did, the Spirit of God hovered over the land, your soul the soil, and brought life from death. A grace. The impenetrable ground softened and opened wide. All that was without form and void took shape. Living water welled up and into the empty spaces. A cloud of burdens lifted above you since they were only ever suitable for the sky to carry. Your eyes a sun now, full of light and a thousand invisible stars. Before long the soil brought forth plants it only received and never planted. Each one came with the discovery of fruit. Of love, kindness, gentleness, patience, self-control, joy, peace, gentleness, and faithfulness. The fruit was proof of your newness. Nothing and everything had changed. You were still a creature but of a different kind. One that recognized your Creator by name and gave Him everything He deserved. The mind and heart you tried to hoard, you gave back. The soul too.

Your newness influenced how you saw the world and everything in it. Creatures looked different. You saw them and remembered who made them. When they hated, you loved. When they were burdened, you took their clouds and carried them toward the sky. You even joined them in praise and prayer for the heaven you shared and the hell you endured on the way.

To be called a new creature is to see your name in the Genesis narrative, but different from it is how you have had two beginnings. One when you were born. The other when you were born again. And this new life has defeated death. That too is different in that it won't be the end of newness but the continuation of it. The end of life will be a kind of beginning, on a new heaven and new earth, where nothing and everything has changed forever.

> For our momentary light affliction is producing for us
> an absolutely incomparable eternal weight of glory.
> So we do not focus on what is seen, but on what is
> unseen. For what is seen is temporary, but what is
> unseen is eternal. 2 CORINTHIANS 4:17-18 CSB

SUFFERING CREATES AN INTERPRETIVE lens. Either refining the sufferer's vision of God or blurring it. An intense but helpful example of this can be observed in Eli Weisel's book *Night*. In it he takes readers through his time in the infamous Auschwitz concentration camp. A version of hell constructed by the human mind, to "house," torture, murder, and use as labor Abraham's children. Weisel describes a scene in which his family steps off the train, onto Auschwitz soil, naive to its origin and intention. His mother and sister are separated from him and his father, never to be seen again. He looks up and sees smoke, a degenerative Mount Zion. He finds where the smoke begins as he watches babies, children, and adults being thrown into fire. The sacrifice of the "weak." At this horror, he writes:

> Never shall I forget that night, the first night in
> camp, that turned my life into one long night

seven times sealed. Never shall I forget that
smoke. Never shall I forget the small faces of the
children whose bodies I saw transformed into
smoke under a silent sky. Never shall I forget
those flames that consumed my faith forever.
Never shall I forget the nocturnal silence that
deprived me for all eternity of the desire to live.
Never shall I forget those moments that murdered
my God and my soul and turned my dreams to
ashes.[3]

Suffering created a lens for Eli that, by the sheer virtue
of its strength, rendered Eli's faith useless and His God
nonexistent. I think about Eli often when I hear about saints
without a holocaust but in relationship with some version of
hell. Their suffering is so wide, so heavy, so unnatural that
it tempts them to deny the truth. Reimagining God functions
as a way to cope with what hurts.

We all do this in some way or another. In degrees usually.
Wherein our circumstances tempt us to doubt something
true about God. That He isn't good or kind, or faithful, or
trustworthy, or present, or powerful or just, or real. The trial
becomes a false teacher to whom we listen because, if we're
honest, believing a lie is more comfortable than reality. Hope
is an uncomfortable project, but to this we are called. And
not without some assurance of its worth. I see Jesus who
borrows from Psalm 22 in His speech to God on Calvary. In
the midst of unimaginable suffering, Jesus speaks to being
forsaken. A circumstance that, from a human perspective,

could easily convey an untruth about God. Jesus leaves the psalm unfinished, but it is available in full for us. After feeling forsaken, David declares the truth:

> My God, my God, why have
>> you forsaken me?
> Why are you so far from saving me,
>> from the words of my groaning?
> . . . *Yet you are holy,*
> enthroned on the praises of Israel.
>> (Ps. 22:1, 3, emphasis added)

Even when life is hard, God is. Even when life is hard, God is good.

Then they despised the pleasant land, having
no faith in his promise. PSALM 106:24

"HOW LONG WILL THEY not believe in me, in spite of all
the signs that I have done among them?" (Num. 14:11). God
said this to Moses after sending twelve spies to Canaan to
observe the land and hearing ten of them come back with a
bad report of it. The report of the ten sounded like this: "The
land, through which we have gone to spy it out, is a land
that devours its inhabitants" (Num. 13:32). And, "we are not
able to go up against the people, for they are stronger than
we are" (Num. 13:31).

Two men who'd gone up with the ten as spies disagreed with
the majority's assessment. They too observed the land and
the men in it. With their own eyes, they saw what they were
up against as a nation, and yet their voice had no quiver in it.
Their hands were still, their spine unwavering. Surely their
courage wasn't an inheritance but a decision. It didn't matter
how tall the people were or how fortified the cities because
as Joshua pleaded, "If the LORD delights in us, he will bring
us into this land and give it to us" (Num. 14:8).

The difference between the two and the ten is this: one group believed God; the other didn't. We don't usually relate courage to faith or fear to unbelief, but considering the spies, it's evident the two had an elevated and thus right view of God that influenced how they perceived the land. For one, they believed He was with them. And He was. God set His affections on this people, determining to rescue them as He promised. After being made free, there was a sea split for them to journey through, and as they journeyed on, from place to place, God was with them day and night. By fire and by cloud. The invisible God becoming visible so His people had an awareness of His care. In addition to this, God instructed Moses on how to build the tabernacle: God *with* His people. He gave them laws to be holy and instructions on how to atone for their failure to do so: God *for* His people. And let's not forget that before the law was given, before the tabernacle was built, before the cloud was before or the fire was behind, God promised to give them this land. The land with people in it that the ten thought were stronger than God. The God who'd come against an entire nation before, but I guess they believed He couldn't do it again.

I'm sad to admit that sometimes we are the two. Most times we are the ten. So awestruck by the bigness of whatever is in front of us that our fears become our lord and king. Like a visitor to a new city, there are signs all around. Follow them and find your place. The brightest of them being a grave with no body in it. The one it was meant for was there, for a moment, and rising from it, He proved His preeminence over it.

By grace, we have been given this same power over death and sin, and therefore, we are strong *too*; God *for* us. By grace, we have been given His spirit. God *with us*.

He who did not spare His own Son, but delivered
Him over for us all, how will He not also with Him
freely give us all things? ROMANS 8:32 NASB

JEHOVAH JIREH HAS A handful of associations. Most
of which have something to do with a phone bill paid, a
good man sent. Dollar bills squeezed into a ball, held in the
hidden palms of a benevolent saint and pushed discreetly
into unsuspecting hands. And this name describes what is
true about Jehovah, the Lord does provide. As He has from
the beginning of everything.

The original ones, Adam and Eve, knew this was the case.
They were created and mandated in an uncultivated yet
ready-made place. They were called to subdue what was
already there. They were told to be fruitful and multiply
with bodies they'd received. Adam named creatures he
didn't create with a mind he didn't make. For anybody to
have or do anything, the Maker of heaven and earth must
provide it. God has always *been*, but Jehovah Jireh as a
description for the eternal One has an origin distinct from
Eden. So, how did this name come to be?

Well, you may recall the story of Abraham and his son Isaac. Called out to go where God would tell him, Abraham was promised that he would be made into a nation, that all families of the earth would be blessed through him and that all of this would come through his seed, Isaac (Gen. 12:1–3; 15:2–5; 17:1–8). Then the plot twists. After Abraham receives this promised child after decades of waiting, God commands him to sacrifice said child (Gen. 22:1–2). This is all a test, but Abraham didn't know that. All he knew, according to Hebrews, was that if God promised Abraham that he would be the Father of many nations and that this promise hinged on Isaac actually being alive, then surely God must have a resurrection up His sleeve (Heb. 11:19).

The time comes for Abraham to obey in Genesis 22:3–10. He and his beloved son go up to Mount Moriah. Issacs's father takes some rope and wraps it around him, the promised son. The son is laid on the wood. The father grabs the knife. The knife is raised, ready to come down on the son. The murder of a promise? Not quite. Before the knife falls, the father hears a voice calling his name. "'Abraham, Abraham!' And he said, 'Here I am'" (Gen. 22:11). The voice says, "Do not lay your hand on the boy or do anything to him, for now I know that you fear God, seeing you have not withheld your son, your only son, from me" (Gen. 22:12). The father looks up, and there in the bush, caught by its horns, is a ram provided as a replacement for the son (Gen. 22:13). In response to the Lord's grace and gift, Abraham memorializes the moment: "So Abraham called the name of that place, 'The LORD will provide'" (Gen. 22:14).

This name, Jireh, calls to mind this moment, when Jehovah Jireh provided a ram in the bush. This moment, a shadow, pointing forward to the day when God would provide His Son in the flesh. Because He was given, the judgment that awaits the wicked, like a knife ready for the neck, fell on the Son as ordained by the Father. There were no rams to replace this son because this Son *was* the substitute for us. He is both the ram in the bush and the Son who resurrects. Glory be to God that He did not withhold His Son, His only Son from us.

"What good will it be for someone to gain the whole
world, yet forfeit their soul?" MATTHEW 16:26 NIV

THE WICKED HAVE IT easy, or so it seems. You see them
because you've been them. You know them by name and
nature. Some of them are friends who preferred the wide
road over the narrow one you left them for. Or family whose
stony hearts ain't moved. By proximity to their lives and
love, you're able to see how life has boded for them, and it
just doesn't seem half bad. Especially for somebody on their
way to hell and all.

Their relationships are steady. The single one found somebody, and you, if single, have prayed and been denied
the same blessing. Other friends never petitioned, never
knocked, never wept like Hannah and got pregnant still.
Some family members hate God, wouldn't dare call Him
good, and yet there's no struggle in their chest. They are
well fed, accomplished; doors open and never close. You
come home and see on TV women and men with millions of
resources. Multiple streams, and you know that you know,
they didn't receive this provision by faith. A delectable

bounty just fell into their throat, while it seems the noose opens and clinches around yours.

Because you, Christian, have been tried by fire. Every few months or days—who knows the time when you're suffering—God makes life hard again. Relationships get weird. Money gets funny. Mind gets confused. Heart gets weary, but the wicked? They wake up every morning with a confounding combination of no fear of God and what looks like all of His favor.

More than one saint in Scripture felt this way too. Jeremiah said: "Why does the way of the wicked prosper? Why do all who are treacherous thrive?" (Jer. 12:1). Job said: "The tents of robbers are at peace, and those who provoke God are secure" (Job 12:6). Malachi said: "And now we call the arrogant blessed. Evildoers not only prosper but they put God to the test and they escape" (Mal. 3:15).

And then there's David who, in Psalm 73, brings attention to what feels like partiality on the part of the Lord (but isn't, for Romans 2:11 makes clear that God shows no partiality). When he considers the hardships of the righteous and the ease of the wicked, he calls attention to the particular temptation of his own heart: "For I was *envious* of the arrogant when I saw the prosperity of the wicked" (v. 3, emphasis added).

David helps us see that one temptation arising during seasons of suffering or lack is envy. What the prophets wanted wasn't just prosperity but the "freedom" it seems to bring. When a saint suffers, naturally what they want most is to be relieved of it. To be comforted, deceptively, by having an easier life. When it is always God's intention for you to learn how to discover comfort in His presence, peace in His care, and freedom by His Spirit. Not in stuff or even in safety but in Him.

What's interesting is how the suffering saints envy because they're distracted. It's only when they turn their gaze from God and look at the wicked that they covet. When they look at *God*, though, they discern. "But when I thought how to understand this, it seemed to me a wearisome task, until I went into the sanctuary of God; then I discerned their end. Truly you set them in slippery places; you make them fall to ruin" (Ps. 73:16–18).

The trials of life might not lift when the suffering saints refocus their gaze, but they become wise as a result. Able to see grace everywhere. Like David who said of himself and God: "I am continually with you" and "My flesh and my heart may fail, but God is the strength of my heart and my portion forever" (vv. 23, 26). If the wicked don't have God, even if they have everything, they have nothing.

Rejoice always, pray without ceasing, give thanks
in all circumstances; for this is the will of God in
Christ Jesus for you. 1 THESSALONIANS 5:16-18

JEALOUSY IS SINISTER IN its origin and destructive in its
application. James said it this way: "But if you have bitter
jealousy and selfish ambition in your hearts, do not boast
and be false to the truth. This is not the wisdom that comes
down from above, but is earthly, unspiritual, demonic. For
where jealousy and selfish ambition exist, there will be
disorder and every vile practice" (James 3:14–16).

Jealousy isn't uncommon for any of us. There's always something somebody has that we want for ourselves. The big
family. The handsome man. The easier life. The doting wife.
The small waist. The big checks. The green grass on the other
side. We compare their blessings (or concealed judgments) to
our own and with the wisdom that comes from below. The
comparison turns competitive.

It's one thing to properly discern what another has that you
don't and find joy in the diversity of God's generosity. And
how He "makes his sun rise on the evil and on the good, and

sends rain on the just and on the unjust" (Matt. 5:45). It's another thing to compare and eventually believe a lie about God and your neighbor because of it. The lie believed of our neighbor is usually that they are unworthy of our joy, our love, our godly praise or even our sincere prayers because of who they are or what they have. See the sinfulness in such a position? It inclines us to disregard the image of God in people and abhor them for being blessed, in some measure, by Him. And then the lie believed about God in one way or another is that He has favorites. That He's been and being more benevolent, kind, or favorable toward another than with you. The truth is, "God shows no partiality" (Rom. 2:11). So your neighbors' blessings aren't because God loves them *more*. It is simply that God in His sovereign wisdom has the right to give to one green grass and to another greener grass. Neither yard suggests more or less care on the part of God.

Another truth is this: "You do not have, because you do not ask. You ask and do not receive, because you ask wrongly, to spend it on your passions" (James 4:2b–3). Some of the things you want, you don't have because you've never asked. Meaning, a pattern of prayerful petition is a way to resist jealousy. If God gave, then God gives. Just in case you do ask and don't receive, consider it as protection. There are some things that God has withheld because what was a blessing for others might be a curse for you. God knows you better than you do. So be careful in coveting gifts you haven't been graced to receive.

Instead, look up, around, and within and grow in thankful-ness for all the good gifts you have received from the Father of Lights. Do you have a body with gifts and a right mind? Tell God, "Thank You." Do you have a Christian community, a family, and a blue sky to live under? Then tell God, "Thank You." Do you have a heart made flesh? A soul made right? And union with Christ? Then tell God, "Thank You."

He was despised and rejected by men, a man of
sorrows and acquainted with grief. ISAIAH 53:3

IN HIS INCARNATION, JESUS became just as needy and
dependent as we are. We all fight so hard to not be vulnerable in this way. What's interesting about it all is that the
projection of needlessness is, in essence, the mimicking of
deity. An attempt to be seen as a god, without needs. We
covet being something more than what we are, and the ironic
part is that the incessant rejection of vulnerability is that,
instead of being something that makes us strong, it ends up
being completely exhausting.

By virtue of His complete humility and in contrast to
every child of Adam, when Christ took on flesh, He chose
weakness. The weaknesses of humanity became His own.
"Though he was in the form of God, did not count equality
with God a thing to be grasped, but emptied himself, by
taking the form of a servant, being born in the likeness of
men" (Phil. 2:6–7). As mysterious as the incarnation is, the
reasons for it are scripturally plain. One explanation is this:
Christ became like you to help you. "Therefore he had to
be made like his brothers in every respect, so that he might

become a merciful and faithful high priest in the service of God, to make propitiation for the sins of the people. For because he himself has suffered when tempted, he is able to help those who are being tempted" (Heb. 2:17–18).

I imagine that the projection of needlessness extends beyond our human relationships, tainting our intimacy with the Father too. We tend to suppose that our closeness to God, holiness, and the like, is all rigidity. Dying to and cutting off. Confession of and repenting for. But what if godliness is elusive (at times) because of our failure to believe that Christ has sympathy? If our image of God is of Him on a throne, looking down on the church His Son redeemed, being weak and fledgling about the world, and in His mind are only criticisms and calculated condemnation, we will naturally withhold our vulnerability from Him, won't we? What would happen, though, if we remembered Jesus in the wilderness being tempted yet victorious? Or Jesus in the garden of Gethsemane suffering yet enduring? Or Jesus in the synagogue being misunderstood but not shrinking? Or Jesus being reviled but not returning it? Or Jesus being betrayed, being tired, being righteously angry, unfairly tried, abandoned, abused, a man of sorrows yet full of joy?

Let's reframe the image now. Keeping the same characters but reconfiguring the plot points. God is there, on the throne, and at His right hand the Son sits. Being fully aware of every weakness and weight and every sin that entangles, the Son doesn't gloat over the failures of the church. For Satan is the accuser of the brethren (Rev. 12:10), but Jesus is their intercessor (Heb. 7:25). Risen from the dead, in the same body, both flesh and deity, Christ as High Priest sees you, and instead of condemnation He offers mercy. This is why the writer of Hebrews *begins* by saying, "For we do not have a high priest who is unable to sympathize with our weaknesses, but one who in every respect has been tempted as we are, yet without sin" *before* saying, "Let us *then* with confidence draw near to the throne of grace, that we may receive mercy and find grace to help in time of need" (Heb. 4:15–16). The empathy precedes the mercy. The sympathy holds hands with grace.

And David said, "The LORD who delivered me from the paw of the lion and from the paw of the bear will deliver me from the hand of this Philistine." 1 SAMUEL 17:37

DAVID REFERENCES HIS PRIOR success with overcoming beasts as the reason he is confident he can overcome Goliath. David has a resume, if you will, and on it, one time he killed a lion. Another time he killed a bear. His statement may seem like an act of boasting. It may appear as if David is so self-assured by his prior experiences with beasts that he assumes fighting Goliath would be easy for him to handle. But David doesn't hand Saul his resume so Saul can trust David only. David gives him his resume as evidence for why he can trust *God* to fight through David. Notice his logic: it's *the Lord* who delivered me back then that will deliver me now. Even though David's name is at the top of his resume, God is the one who did all the work.

Speaking of work, we're in a super-ambitious era. We may not be killing lions and tigers and bears, but we are killing it. Interestingly enough, though productivity is at an all-time high, so is anxiety, which is another form of fear. I think one part of the collective increase in anxiety in our current era is because we've become incredibly efficient in accomplishing a thousand tasks all the time. We are raising babies and getting degrees and eating jackfruit pulled-pork sandwiches and listening to podcasts and exfoliating our pores—all while trying to serve in church and read the Bible and resist the world, the flesh, and the devil. We are working hard, and we have produced a lot to prove it.

However. When we look at our resumes and see ourselves and all that we've accomplished instead of God's grace, then when something doesn't go according to plan, or work like it used to, when the strategies that have always worked for us turn around and fail us, we cope with the anxiety of it all by trying to be more productive instead of becoming more humble. We strategize before praying. We work before resting. We even cut out rest altogether sometimes. All because when you know that you know that you know how to get stuff done, you start believing you are the common denominator in every victory. You start thinking it's not *the Lord* who delivered you last time and will deliver you this time but you.

What if some of our fear and our angst and stress is a consequence of us making an idol out of our ability to produce? Imagine if David heard Goliath popping at the mouth and rightly remembered that he'd already fought things that were bigger than him but then forgot to trace his previous victory to God; David would've been walking in the same pride Goliath walked in. And how does God respond to proud people? The Bible says He resists them. David was not about to defeat a giant with his ego. And neither can you. He would only succeed in the fight if God fought for him.

Those who cling to worthless idols forfeit the
grace that could be theirs. JONAH 2:8 NIV1984

SURRENDER IS A SCARY word. If you're anything like
me, your heart moves every time you hear it because you're
aware of all that is in you or in your life that might need
to go, to leave, to be tossed up toward heaven and given to
God. Surrender ain't a new word though. Or should I say a
new concept.

In Genesis, you have two people, Adam and Eve, who were
made in the image of God and thus for His glory, who by
virtue of their perfection lived in a continual state of surrender. Where their bodies, and their lives were always *His*.
And by His, I mean God's. They lived for Him.

Until, of course, the serpent showed up. The devil didn't try
to delete the concept of surrender however. He didn't tell
them they shouldn't surrender at all. All he did was put them
in the position to surrender to something or someone other
than God. Where their bodies and their lives were given over
to the glory of a created thing instead of the Creator. Through
temptation and deception, they were willing to sacrifice their

entire selves on somebody else's altar because they stopped believing that God was the worthy one.

This same reasoning is in us. That's why surrender scares us, because we think that if we give up what God is telling us to give Him—if we hand Him that thing that means too much, if we just decide to stop bowing down at the foot of the idols of our own making and stand on our two feet—we will be lacking something. We reckon that to surrender to God is to relinquish our joy, and what an ancient lie that is. The lie being that once my hands are open and empty, God isn't big enough or good enough to fill them up again. Our fear of surrender is really our unbelief that God isn't better than everything God is asking us to give Him. You will give God anything when you believe He is everything.

Funny thing, Jesus has been there, done that. Not counting equality with God a thing to be grasped, He emptied Himself because the Father was everything to Him. Think about that again. Jesus, God of heaven, Lord of everything, became a servant because the Father was everything to Him. The invisible King was born in the likeness of men because God was everything to Him. And then the Lord of glory was found in human form and became obedient to the point of death because God was everything to Him. And after it all, the Father "highly exalted him and bestowed on him the name that is above every name, so that at the name of Jesus every knee should bow, in heaven and on earth and under the earth, and every tongue confess that Jesus Christ is Lord, to the glory of God the Father" (Phil. 2:9–11).

The point is this: there is nothing in your hands that God won't replace with more of Himself. So let it go. Let it fly. Let it burn. God is better anyway. It might hurt. It might suck. You might miss it. You might have to sacrifice some things. Confess some stuff. But on the other side of surrender is God. And I don't know about you, but I'd rather have Him more than anything because He is better than everything.

Death and life are in the power of the tongue, and those who love it will eat its fruits. PROVERBS 18:21

THERE'S A MUSEUM OF swords in Scripture. One that pierces through bone and marrow, flesh and blood, in a particular way, is this one: "And the tongue is a fire, a world of unrighteousness. . . . With it we bless our Lord and Father, and with it we curse people who are made in the likeness of God. From the same mouth come blessing and cursing. My brothers, these things ought not to be so" (James 3:6, 9–10). As it broke flesh, the blood proved the pain. The body felt the knife, and the heart hurt at the sound of it. Contradiction is noisy, ain't it?

How James sees it, as moved along by the Spirit, the way we speak to and about people tells a story. If we understand everyone, friend and foe, neighbor and nuisance, as made in the likeness of God, the words we say should be tempered by that truth. Every single person we will ever converse with, both sinner and saint, bears the image of God; and for that reason, each person is worthy of honor.

Or as C. S. Lewis would put it:

> The dullest most uninteresting person you can talk
> to may one day be a creature which, if you saw it
> now, you would be strongly tempted to worship,
> or else a horror and a corruption such as you now
> meet, if at all, only in a nightmare. . . . There are no
> ordinary people. You have never talked to a mere
> mortal. . . . But it is immortals whom we joke with,
> work with, marry, snub, and exploit—immortal
> horrors or everlasting splendors.[4]

To reiterate the thought, if God made everyone, everyone
is special. Not only does the nature of our neighbor matter,
as far as our words are concerned, but our words reveal
the integrity of our inner self. Or rather the disintegration
between the two when our words demonstrate an obvious
combination of both blessing and cursing out of the same
mouth. James calls our attention to our inconsistency here
by explaining that a plant's fruit should correspond with the
plant's nature:

> Does a spring pour forth from the same opening
> both fresh and salt water? Can a fig tree, my
> brothers, bear olives, or a grapevine produce figs?
> Neither can a salt pond yield fresh water. (James
> 3:11–12)

Someone might attempt to fix the problem of the tongue by
simply refusing to talk, but silence doesn't regenerate or
sanctify. To tame the tongue, we have to actually deal with
who we are. "Out of the abundance of the heart [the] mouth

speaks" (Luke 6:45). By dealing with not just the words we say but also the heart that determines the speech, we can work toward the unity of our words and our worship.

Do not be misled: "Bad company corrupts
good character." 1 CORINTHIANS 15:33 NIV

IN PSALM 1, THE psalmist pronounces blessing on the ones who watch where they walk, sit, and stand, making sure neither is done around the wicked and sinful. We might be distracted by the verbs and try to find some revelation between the letters. But it really is as simple as it seems: "Blessed is the man who walks not in the counsel of the wicked, nor stands in the way of sinners, nor sits in the seat of scoffers" (Ps. 1:1).

This is to say, blessed is the woman who refuses the voice of friends who love the earth more than the kingdom above it. Those friends who are a choir of darkness. Who steal Satan's sentences and call it "advice."

This is to say, blessed is the man who won't step on certain soil. He's seen the kinds of trees that grow from it. Fruitless yet familiar. He's been one before, a branch with no roots. A man with no joy. The carrier of a big mouth and a thirsty soul, hunting the daughters of men like a hungry ghost. He's gone that way and didn't see God at the end of it.

This is to say, blessed is the woman who is uninterested in drinking iced lattes with scoffing scoffers. It's a perversion of the intellect, you know? To take what God has revealed and use the mind He gave, with the heart Adam determined, and fix one's mouth to call God anything other than Lord.

The scoffing scoffers host parties, write books, lead classrooms, engage in discussion, with doubt stuck in their throat. They mock Jesus and the ones who love Him. Unforgiven is the one who blasphemes. Blessed is the one who believes instead.

In response, the psalmist doesn't suggest a better crowd to hang around as an alternative (which is wisdom of course); rather, he says: "But his delight is in the law of the LORD, and on his law he meditates day and night" (Ps. 1:2). The ways and words we engage with during our day can function as a form of meditation. Whether it's an endless scroll throughout the day, gazing at certain people we don't know who don't love God, consistent engagement in that certain thread of worldly friends, or binging on that certain series we know elevates godless living, if our mind is in the constant presence of the counsel of the wicked, way of sinners, and seat of scoffers, then naturally, our lives will be formed by it. We will think as they do. Walk as they walk. Sit where they sit. Deciding against all that is indeed an act of discipline, but such discipline can only be sustained by the heart taking *joy* in what the will chose. Meditating on God's Law day and night is a holy consequence of first delighting in it. God's Word offers paths of walking that lead to life. Ways of being that promote peace. And places to sit where Jesus as Lord is a welcomed song.

For am I now seeking the approval of man,
or of God? Or am I trying to please man? If
I were still trying to please man, I would not
be a servant of Christ. GALATIANS 1:10

HUMILITY MAKES ME CURIOUS. It's a foreign way of being
for everybody but God. As gigantic as Jesus's life was, He
was small in it. Or to say it another way, in the Gospels, you
see the Creator of everything willfully minimizing Himself
to the point that He is sometimes unnoticeable.

Take His first miracle for example. There's a wedding. Jesus
is there with His disciples. His mother too. Wine is poured,
drunk, then all gone. Mary asks Jesus to help, and He does,
but not in the way anybody might expect. The servants fill
jars with water at Jesus's command. Then they are told to
draw some out and deliver it to the master of the feast. The
water, now wine, is tasted and praised as being better than
the first. But have you ever noticed who was praised and how
it wasn't Jesus? The master of the feast has no idea he just
swallowed a miracle. Most of the party doesn't either. For all
they know, the bridegroom was being an excellent host. All
the goodness they drank poured out of them and toward the

one for whom it didn't belong. Meanwhile the maker of the wine and the world stood in the room completely content with not just sharing His glory but releasing it completely to someone who didn't deserve the credit.

When is the last time you did good without expecting, hoping, or suggesting it be noticed? When you gave, served, prayed, fasted, studied, rejoiced, taught, died to, wiped, cooked, cleaned, labored for, organized, plucked out, cut out, built up anything, did you expect a parade? When it didn't come, how did it leave you? Bitter? Discouraged? Both, maybe? Could it be that the expectation belongs to an invisible pride? The kind that leaves us unsatisfied by the gaze of God. The kind that makes us the "they" in John 12:43: "For they loved the glory that comes from man more than the glory that comes from God."

How much of our "goodness" is, if we really took the time to dig it up and look, grown out of the soil of an insatiable need to be loved and liked by people that didn't create us? Their praise is immediate and felt, whereas God glorying in us is an act of faith in what He had said and will say.

Read Jesus's words and believe them: "Beware of practicing your righteousness before other people in order to be seen by them, for then you will have no reward from your Father who is in heaven. Thus, when you give to the needy, sound no trumpet before you, as the hypocrites do in the synagogues and in the streets, that they may be praised by others. Truly, I say to you, they have received their reward.

But when you give to the needy, do not let your left hand know what your right hand is doing, so that your giving may be in secret. And your Father who sees in secret will reward you" (Matt. 6:1–4).

Beloved, Jesus commands us to do as He does. Turn the water to wine, let them drink, watch them rejoice in it, and if they leave your name out of their song, that's okay. There's a better praise awaiting you.

For they provoked him to anger with their high places;
they moved him to jealousy with their idols. PSALM 78:58

FIRST QUESTION: DO WE know an idol when we see it?
Paul did. "Now while Paul was waiting for them at Athens,
his spirit was provoked within him as he saw that the city
was full of idols" (Acts 17:16). What Paul saw as idols,
we enter a museum and call "art," which could stand as
a contemporary metaphor in this way. We are constantly
discerning the proper descriptions of things. Whether to call
it art or an idol, a family or a god, a job or a lord, money or
master. Aaron made a *golden calf*. Art. They called it *god*.
Idolatry. And the way to determine if a thing is one or the
other is to pay attention to the way people handle it.

The Athenians called their gods *gods* and treated them
as such. We call the things we worship by normal names,
hence the reason we view ourselves less idolatrous than
the ancients. You can go to the east of this American nation
and encounter one thousand gods on one train ride. You
can travel to the west, where Hollywood's throne sits, high
and lifted up, and see the beautiful ones. You'd have to be
discerning to know that "Pretty" is the lord among them.

Find your way to the South, and you might just think it's God's country. When in fact, the country is god.

Turn to the right and to the left, and indeed, every city is full of idols. But, *but*, even if this is true—another question after the first is, Do you care? Paul's spirit was "provoked" (Acts 17:16). Agitated. Moved to emotion. It's one thing to know evil when you see it; it's another to have a spirit that's provoked because of it. Moses saw the idol known as a golden calf and his "anger burned hot, and he threw the tablets out of his hands and broke them at the foot of the mountain" (Exod. 32:19). When Jesus saw men, with hearts like cities, full of idols, "he looked around at them with anger, grieved at their hardness of heart" (Mark 3:5). I'd argue that godly provocation is a by-product of a right view of both God and man that impresses upon the heart both grief and anger, lament and compassion.

Last question. When Paul addresses the idolatry he observes (which is to say that provocation should motivate instruction), how does he do it? He lifts up the nature of God. "For as I passed along and observed the objects of your worship, I found also an altar with this inscription: 'To the unknown god.' What therefore you worship as unknown, this I proclaim to you. The God who made the world and everything in it, being Lord of heaven and earth, does not live in temples made by man, nor is he served by human hands, as though he needed anything" (Acts 17:23–25). Which frames for the idolatrous ones the illegitimacy of their, and our, objects of worship. And Paul also makes clear the nature of man: "In him we live and move and have our being" (v. 28). Which puts forward our entire existence as being completely dependent on God who is Lord of heaven and earth. Therefore, the sustenance we believe an idol provided was actually from God's hand alone. And finally, Paul addresses the Creator's purpose for man: "And he made from one man every nation of mankind to live on all the face of the earth, having determined allotted periods and the boundaries of their dwelling place, that they should seek God, and perhaps feel their way toward him and find him" (vv. 26–27). So then, our reason for being made and placed where we are, from the East to the West, is so that we will find God. When we find Him, we will know it when we see it.

And the LORD sent Nathan to David. 2 SAMUEL 12:1

EVERYBODY NEEDS A NATHAN. Someone sent with a courageous love and a wise set of words for the benefit of our faith. How else would David have seen himself?

We know the story in 2 Samuel 12, don't we? David walked his roof; looking below it and seeing Bathsheba, he summoned her to himself. When he learned about the seed he planted, he schemed to cover the sin. A false atonement. He settled on murdering her husband Uriah and succeeded. Bathsheba carried and birthed the child and not once did David confess. Between the summoning and the birth, almost a year had passed. Blindness ages with us unless God sends someone to help us see again. Like Peter who denied Jesus three times and didn't grieve until a rooster crowed.

Nathan comes and tells David a story about a rich man with many flocks and a poor man with only one lamb. A guest of the rich man comes, and instead of practicing hospitality out of his own abundance, the man takes the only lamb the poor man has. David hears the story and rage rises within. Such emotion could be perceived as righteous anger. If he were a preacher, you might be led to believe his passion was symbolic of his purity, but somewhere in a room was the woman he stole. Somewhere in a grave was the poor man he stole her from.

His sins were real and obvious, and yet David's convictions were angled at imaginary wickedness. In response to the story, David says: "As the Lord lives, the man who has done this deserves to die" (2 Sam. 12:5). David discerned what should be done to the man, but he failed to see himself as the one it should be done to. "Nathan said to David, 'You are the man!'" (v. 7).

Everybody needs a Nathan. Without one, two, and many, we will discern truth to a degree. We will have some meager insight to perceive justice, righteousness, truth, and how they should and shouldn't be expressed. However, articulating what is *right* isn't the evidence of present righteousness. We can't even discern that if we only look to ourselves as confirmation about ourselves. It's more than possible to be accurate and righteous in our judgment of other men while ignorant of the ways we mirror them.

Everybody needs a Nathan. Someone who will love us enough to tell us the truth. Who will see the plank between blinks and do the careful work of helping us remove it.

Everybody needs a Nathan. Someone God has sent our way as a merciful missionary. The psalmist said: "Let a righteous man strike me—it is a kindness; let him rebuke me—it is oil for my head; let my head not refuse it" (Ps. 141:5).

Everybody needs a Nathan.

So when the woman saw that the tree . . . was a delight to the eyes, . . . she took of its fruit and ate. GENESIS 3:6

THE MAGIC OF BEAUTY is how it pulls us toward itself. Whenever we find it in anything, we want it to last. To stay, with us usually.

The invention of a phone that doubles as a camera brought our love for beauty to the surface. How many of us, when seated at dinner, hungry as ever, commit to a momentary fast just to photograph our plate? We not only want to remember what we saw, even before it was tasted, but we also want to share it. What's the point of beauty if we can't tell somebody about it? "Girl, have you seen her baby? She's gorgeous!" "Bro, these shoes fire, ain't they?" "Mommy look! It's a rainbow!" No wonder Eve ate the fruit and immediately gave it away to her husband.

The trouble with beauty is never the beautiful thing itself. Just as it was with the fruit Eve thought was to die for, it's *us*. God, most beautiful, has gifted us color, food, music, friends, smiles, language, as extensions of His inherent loveliness. "Every good gift and every perfect gift is from above" (James 1:17). And so, having hearts that Jeremiah called "deceitfully wicked," our problem isn't necessarily that we can't discern beauty; it's that we are so nearsighted we can't recognize the transcendent beauty that all of our earthly attractions are intended to move us *toward*. Or, as Hannah Anderson would put it, "Beautiful things draw us beyond themselves to a reality greater than either of us."[5]

Laughter is beautiful, right? We make it our business to create space for it and build relationships around it. The experience of it is a spectacle. The mouth opens, tears fall, hands may flail, all kinds of incoherent sounds escape us, and every expression is just joy entering the body. That is beautiful. But this beauty has a source that exists beyond the laughter itself. Intimacy is beautiful too, right? When hands hold, bodies hug, a forehead is kissed, a friend arrives and listens the whole time. It is a beautiful thing to be known and still loved. The entire world chases this, but in an inordinate way. It prefers the shadow over the substance.

How many songs, movies, and addictions exist because we are chasing a beautiful thing and completely blind to where all the beauty came from? How many souls entered hell because they didn't believe the Creator was more beautiful than everything He'd made? We'd do well to trace all beauty to its origin. All joy to its maker. Every intimacy to its Creator. Today's love to its source.

As we were going to the place of prayer, we were
met by a slave girl who had a spirit of divination and
brought her owners much gain by fortune-telling.
She followed Paul and us, crying out, "These men
are servants of the Most High God, who proclaim
to you the way of salvation." And this she kept
doing for many days. Paul, having become greatly
annoyed, turned and said to the spirit, "I command
you in the name of Jesus Christ to come out of
her." And it came out that very hour. ACTS 16:16-18

IN OUR ANNOYANCE WITH people we love or strongly
dislike, we often discern their behavior through an earthly
lens. In one way, we should, since we are in the flesh (as
in, fallen), and they are too. If and when they are jealous,
covetous, unloving, and every other sin done by everybody
but God, then that too is a product of the flesh (the sinful
nature).

And yet, Scripture also says, "For we do not wrestle against
flesh and blood, but against the rulers, against the authorities,
against the cosmic powers over this present darkness, against

the spiritual forces of evil in the heavenly places" (Eph. 6:12). Meaning that a spiritual reality influences the behavior of everyone we meet. To those who walk by the Spirit, their kindness, gentleness, patience, and other good fruit are the Holy Spirit's doing. To those who live according to the flesh, Jesus's word applies: "You are of your father the devil, and your will is to do your father's desires" (John 8:44).

What's my point? That sometimes people's terrible behavior is simply because of their own fleshly nature as fallen human beings, and other times it's because of the enemy's direct (or indirect) influence. What strikes me in Acts 16 regarding all this is that Paul heard the girl's voice but spoke to the spirit in her. He didn't disparage *her* but clearly condemned the thing *behind* her maddening actions. He remembered that there was more going on in the people around him than just what meets the eye.

Now hear me. None of this is to say we should assume that all disagreements or difficult interactions are because of demon possession. Or that exorcism is the ideal when a simple conversation, or removing the log out of our eyes, or dealing with our own fleshly fallenness might be the wiser option. It is to say that if there is more to reality than flesh and blood, then we should pray more than we do, lean into the Holy Spirit more than we have, and show more grace to everyone more than we'd like. Even when people are antagonistic toward us or annoying us beyond words. For even if they are an enemy, they are not *the enemy.*

I am sure of this, that he who started a good
work in you will carry it on to completion until
the day of Christ Jesus. PHILIPPIANS 1:6 CSB

DISCOURAGEMENT IS A TYPICAL experience for most believers. Especially the ones with any kind of self-awareness. We read the Scriptures, see the Son, and don't see ourselves. When Paul says things like, "Follow me as I follow Christ" (1 Cor. 11:1 MEV), we chuckle with insecurity. Every morning, there are new mercies and the same us, or so we think. Our weaknesses and slow growth are ever before us, as a reminder of how far we have to go in looking like Jesus.

God knows this about us, that we need Him to become like Him. So in response to our need, He prunes the branches. A trial here. Some suffering there. So that we can be refined by the fire and made holy because of it. What we often neglect to contemplate is how our response to trials is now and how different our responses are or aren't from our responses then. Charles Spurgeon said:

> The Lord knows how to educate you up to such a
> point that you can endure in years to come what
> you could not endure today; just as today He may

make you to stand firm under a burden, which, ten years ago, would have crushed you into the dust.[6]

When the Lord commanded Abraham to sacrifice Isaac, it was a test, which we know. It wasn't Abraham's first test, however. Do you remember what God commanded Abraham to do when he called him in Genesis 12? He told him to leave his country, his family, and his home and go where God wanted him to go. Therefore, Abraham was well acquainted with God telling him to sacrifice something he loves. No wonder the text has no mention of Abraham resisting God's will, like a Jonah. In God's providential care of Abraham, he'd readied his faith so that as each test increased in intensity, Abraham's stamina did too. Each opportunity to endure benefited his endurance, and we know that "endurance produces character" (Rom. 5:4).

So in the middle of the next trial, pay attention to your response. How's your faith in it, your joy during it, your resolve because of it? I'm sure it won't be as perfect as the Christ's, but is it better than what it used to be? Is it moving you more toward Christ than you were the last go-around? If so, be encouraged. God is completing a work in you. Morning by morning and day by day, the mercies aren't the only new thing you're waking up to. It's also you.

O LORD, you have searched me and known me!
You know when I sit down and when I rise up;
you discern my thoughts from afar.
You search out my path and my lying down
and are acquainted with all my ways.
Even before a word is on my tongue,
behold, O LORD, you know it altogether. PSALM 139:1-4

DEPENDING ON WHO YOU are, or should I say, depending on how you live, the saying "God knows my heart" may land a particular way. There are those who use the sentence as justification for lawless behavior, supposing God sees their pure intentions even when the behavior is obviously unclean. It's a way to numb the conscience and harden the heart. Which is most ironic, for Christ offers His blood to cleanse the conscience and soften the heart.

There are others for whom that statement gives rise to a spirit of fear. Simply because they know their heart too. If it were a house, they know the design of each room and how it looks nothing like heaven. Interrogating your own self has its benefits, but along with it is the temptation of self-deprecation. Seeing sin in yourself can elicit much shame, so imagine reckoning with the Holy One seeing you and your heart with transcendent clarity. You will either hide from His glare in self-condemnation or through self-deceit.

Read today's passage again. How does it make you feel? Insecure? Safe? Exposed? Maybe all of it at once and in different degrees? The project of our day-to-day life is projecting versions of ourselves as protection. We've created different ways of being a shield against being seen as ourselves. We don't want people to know who we really are. How weak and inadequate we really feel. How goofy or silly we can actually become when joy removes the mask. Being a part of certain religious institutions helps us hide in plain sight. Depending on the spiritual gift for which you've been graced, it can function as a way to build up the body *and* as a building to shelter yourself from it. Preach, sing, lead, organize, exhort, or pray good enough, and people might believe you're an angel in disguise. When in fact, you're just a human afraid to be free.

Hiding from the truth of our sin and ourselves doesn't serve us or our neighbor in the long run. The Lord, who knows each sentence before it's said and each action before it's done, is also the same Lord who "formed [your] inward parts" and "knitted [you] together in [your] mother's womb" (Ps. 139:13). He has an intimate knowledge of you and loves you still. The depth to which God sees you offers security for when no one else does. In your hiding, you remain unknown, and yet you are well known by God. When you want to hide, remember Christ, who covers your shame so that you don't have to hide from it. When you want to be something other than who you are, call to mind that you are "fearfully and wonderfully made" (v. 14). Yes, the Lord knows your heart and everything else about you, but knowing *His* heart will set you free to be you and to be His.

Even though I walk through the valley
of the shadow of death,
I will fear no evil, for you are with me;
your rod and your staff, they comfort me. . . .
Surely goodness and mercy shall follow me
all the days of my life, and I shall dwell in the
house of the LORD forever. PSALM 23:4, 6

WHEN DAVID SAYS, "I will fear no evil," what comes to mind? Does the word *evil* stand out and raise its hand? The word has an extreme vibe to us, doesn't it? As if it should only represent the extremes of darkness. The devil, demons, and whatever come close to it. But when we see evil simply as the inverse of good, then the definition opens wide.

By evil, David means both wickedness and adversity. Darkness and injustice. Danger and depression. Badness and betrayal. David walks through the valley of the shadow of death, aware of evil, and refuses to fear it. This is an unfamiliar courage for many of us since we fear evil even when there aren't any shadows. In our friendships we fear evil. That's why we refuse intimacy or anything like it. We fear the evil of betrayal, of judgment, of disappointing them or being disappointed by them, of love being given and then taken away.

When anxiety hovers over us like a cloud of worry, it is because we fear the potential evils of the future. When anger settles in us, refusing joy, it is because we fear the lack of immediate retribution as a form of evil that only *our* anger can resolve. Unforgiveness is an expression of such a fear. The angst being that if I release them of the offense, the offender will be freed to do evil toward us again. Unforgiveness, vengeance, and being guarded won't keep you from evil though; it will instead cultivate evil in you. Not fearing evil isn't an activity by which we live in a dream world where evil is no longer a possibility. Where sinners are, evil is too.

David resisted fear by being secure in God's presence and protection. You don't have to fear evil when the always good God walks with you. He says for "you are with me; your rod and your staff, they comfort me." Which brings to mind David, the shepherd boy who killed a giant with the same items he used to protect his sheep. The resources the good God used to protect you are the same resources He will use to fight for you. Much of what we fear is so because our conviction about who walks with us is shallow. We are in need of intimacy and revelation in the knowledge of Him wherein we believe *we walk with God.* A good One at that. We are invited to believe that He is the Lord of hosts and the warrior of heaven. That in being for us, no one can be against us.

Courage is a by-product of faith. Which isn't a feeling or a mere affection but the commitment to trusting in the *good* Shepherd. Hoping in Him more than anything opens us up to the freedom of believing the best about our life. Instead of fearing evil, we can expect good. And that it will *surely* follow us all of our days.

And we are his house, if indeed we hold fast our confidence. . . .Take care, brothers, lest there be in any of you an evil, unbelieving heart, leading you to fall away from the living God. But exhort one another every day, as long as it is called "today," that none of you may be hardened by the deceitfulness of sin. HEBREWS 3:6B, 12-13

WHEN ISRAEL ENTERED THE wilderness and saw no water in it, they weren't happy campers. Pun intended. The text says the people quarreled with Moses saying, "Why did you bring us up out of Egypt, to kill us and our children and our livestock with thirst?" (Exod. 17:3). Intense, right?

I wonder how different the story might've been if they chose to exhort one another on the faithfulness of God. Let's reimagine the story as one that ends in faith, not sin. Let's say after they walk in the wilderness all day, they end up camping out at Rephidim, and notice, naturally, how thirsty they are. Looking around, they don't see any lakes, rivers, wells, nothing. Meaning the wilderness doesn't have any natural sources of water. Which might be discouraging if they believe their survival is dependent on their environment and not their God, but since that's not the case, they choose to rehearse God's faithfulness. They talk among themselves about how it wasn't that long ago that they were thirsty in the wilderness of Shur—about how when they found water and couldn't drink it 'cause it was bitter, God made it sweet.

And then, let's say since these Israelites are already in remembrance mode, they choose to rehearse another story of their history. They recall that time they were fleeing Egypt and got to a body of water they couldn't swim through, only to find that God parted the sea so they could walk on dry land.

And while they're at it, let's say they keep going, recalling how, if their memory serves them right, the first plague God did among them in Egypt was turning the rivers, the canals, and every single source of water in Egypt into blood.

If Israel had done this—if they had meditated on every story long enough and thought about the truth more than their thirst—they would've had the confidence to believe that if God could curse water, and sweeten water, and split water, then surely He could create water where there is none. But that's neither here nor there.

If only the Israelites exhorted one another on what's true, they would've had the assurance needed to trust God. But there was no exhortation, no faith, no mention of all the glory God had already revealed. Just unbelief. All this is why the writer of Hebrews said: "But exhort one another every day, as long as it is called 'today,' that none of you may be hardened by the deceitfulness of sin" (3:13). Without exhortation, we are prone to let the different discomforts in our body, mind, and environment influence our faith. But when exhortation is present within the mouth of a friend, the body of a sermon, or the bridge of a worship song, our hearts are reminded that God is faithful. And we are so easily discouraged that we need to be encouraged, by the truth, every single day.

What would happen if you experienced exhortation in the valley and on the mountaintop? On Sunday morning and Tuesday afternoon? You'd remember His past deeds done on your behalf. And you'd have the courage to trust that God can and will always make ways out of no way.

"Work, for I am with you, declares
the LORD of hosts." HAGGAI 2:4

GOD BEING WITH US in ministry motivates mission.
Consider how many commissions included the promise
of presence. To Jacob, Moses, Joshua, Jeremiah, God says,
in effect, "Go do this and I will be with you." Then Jesus,
in Matthew 28:19–20, commissions the disciples and says,
"Go therefore and make disciples of all nations, . . . teaching
them to obey all that I have commanded you, and guess
what, I will be with you."

The failure to believe God is with us in ministry affects us
in more ways than one. On one hand, the issue isn't raising
up a generation bold enough to go to the nations to make
disciples—they'll go—they're just afraid to teach all that
God commanded once they get there. And I get it, I get it.
Nobody wants to be an outcast, or hated or unfollowed, or
unloved, unliked for their faith. But if your fear of people
discourages you from being faithful to the text and to God,
then somewhere in there you don't believe God is with you.

On the other hand, there's a common frustration among the faithful. They have planted seeds as often as they know how, into whatever soil they've been called to till with whatever gift they've been graced to use, and the evidence of their labor tarries. The truth they tell is resisted. The exhortation they provide is rejected. Meanwhile, they're so discouraged by the slow fruitfulness of ministry that they are unable to trust the invisible work the Spirit is doing underground. God is with the one who plants, for without Him, no amount of ministry work would take root. "So neither he who plants nor he who waters is anything, but only God who gives the growth" (1 Cor. 3:7).

How many temptations exist because we believe that in all our doing we are actually alone? *God is with you.* And by God I mean the Creator of heaven and earth. The Alpha and the Omega, the beginning and the end. The supreme One. The King of glory. The Judge of all the earth. The immutable and transcendent God. The Lord of hosts. If *that* God is with us, we should be the most confident people on the planet.

Do you understand the kind of confidence you'd have in your ministry if you believed this? It's the kind of confidence that would produce power. The power needed for an effective and durable ministry that obeys *all* the components of the Great Commission. We often pray for the power to *do* in ministry forgetting that we also need the power to *last.* It takes as much power to tell the truth in love as it does to endure suffering for it. Faith in the nearness of God creates the resilience needed to keep leading, loving, giving, evangelizing, serving, praying for, and preaching to.

Beloved, remember Paul, who experienced the distinct suffering of ministry, like loneliness, but he knew that, in reality, he wasn't alone. "At my first defense no one came to stand by me, but all deserted me. May it not be charged against them! But the Lord stood by me and strengthened me" (2 Tim. 4:16–17). The same strength is available to all those who have been commissioned by the Lord Jesus. As we go, He is with us.

And after six days Jesus took with him Peter and
James and John, and led them up a high mountain
by themselves. And he was transfigured before them,
and his clothes became radiant, intensely white, as
no one on earth could bleach them. MARK 9:2-3

ON THIS MOUNTAIN IN Mark 9, the Lord in flesh decided
to transfigure in front of John, Peter, and James. Seeing Him,
they saw Him as He is. Full of glory and light. A color like
bleach but not. Something like white but not. An indescrib-
able moment that became more fantastic when Moses and
Elijah eventually appeared with Him (v. 4).

You would expect the disciples to remain silent, arrested by
the unbelievability of the moment. Then a voice, a familiar
one, interjected: "And Peter said to Jesus, 'Rabbi, it is good
that we are here. Let us make three tents, one for you and one
for Moses and one for Elijah.' For he did not know what to
say, for they were terrified" (Mark 9:5–6). Oh Peter, always
putting sentences where they don't belong. This was typical
of Peter, so I'm sure not one of the disciples were surprised
by the comment. He's the one who saw the Lord walk on
water and asked to do the same, sinking three steps into

the wave (Matt.14:22–31). He's the one who rebuked Jesus (Matt. 16:22). He's the one who would eventually say he'd die before denying the Christ (Matt. 26:35), and not too long after, he denied the Christ (Matt. 26:69–75). Peter's way with words was as wild as the waters he barely walked on.

From the outside looking in, we probably see ourselves in the consistency of Peter's failures. Especially failures that seem to be suitable to his particular personality. The introverted among us may not be as impulsive with their words, but they carry specific temptations. How we exist—meaning, our wiring or personality—tends to influence the way we struggle. The creative has the imagination to make something out of nothing but also to make something out of nothing. The thinker can think but can he also believe? How many intellectuals do we know who will not let God into their mind because it isn't big enough to hold Him?

And so the sins arising from Peter's nature are relatable. But with that they can also be burdensome. It can feel as if particular failures are so specific to who you are that the thought of doing better is impossible unless you *become* different. Which is true. "As [a man] thinketh in his heart, so is he" (Prov. 23:7 KJV). Becoming is hard but it isn't impossible. It is only out of reach for those who imagine their own transfiguration as coming from within instead of from without.

On the day of Pentecost, 120 folks were gathered in one place, including Peter. A sound from heaven filled the space, tongues of fire appeared above them, and out of each of them came sentences from the Spirit in languages they'd never learned. As they spoke, they were mocked. When no one spoke up, the impulsive, rebuking, and denying Peter stood up and showed himself as the bold, courageous, and truth-telling Peter God commissioned him to be. And the text says, "And with many other words he bore witness" (Acts 2:40). The very part of Peter that caused him to fail was the very part God used.

Our personalities aren't in the way of our fruitfulness; sin is. The comprehensive nature of it influences the harshness of our speech or the intensity of our hustle. But when we, like Peter, behold the glory of Jesus and are filled with the Spirit of holiness, we discover God and ourselves. What condemned us before becomes useful for mission now. Thanks be to God that in Christ's redemption, He cleansed and clarified not only what you are but who you are.

So Sarah laughed to herself, saying, "After I am worn out, and my lord is old, shall I have pleasure?" The LORD said to Abraham, "Why did Sarah laugh and say, 'Shall I indeed bear a child, now that I am old?' Is anything too hard for the LORD?" GENESIS 18:12-14A

SARAH'S WOMB HAD BEEN closed for so long that even the suggestion, from the Lord Himself, that the child God promised was on the way, made her chuckle.

The Word of God makes claims that can feel so fantastic we don't know whether to cry or laugh. Super-other-worldly, this-can't-be-true, this-is-crazy kinda statements like, "Now to him who is able to do far more abundantly than all that we ask or think, according to the power at work within us" (Eph. 3:20–21). Or, "There is therefore now no condemnation for those who are in Christ Jesus" (Rom. 8:1). And, "See what kind of love the Father has given to us, that we should be called children of God; and so we are" (1 John 3:1).

Those verses are used often, quoted regularly, and preached powerfully, but sincere faith in it is hard to find sometimes. Consider the shallowness of our prayers and how it might reflect unbelief in God's ability to do abundantly above what the mind thinks or what the mouth prays. How many days do we let shame speak a word over us because of some well-deserved guilt that Christ took care of already? The simple promises tend to be the hardest to believe.

That's because doubt often feels more practical than believing God. God's promise of granting a son to Sarah wasn't complicated. He told Abraham, "I will surely return to you about this time next year, and Sarah your wife shall have a son" (Gen. 18:10). Sarah's long life with a barren womb and the reality of her aging to the degree that the natural possibility of pregnancy was so far out of her reach that she'd started to believe it was out of God's too. That's another trait of unbelief, you know? Projection. We become so aware of our own inability to change circumstances or even ourselves that we imagine God must be as we are. You may begin to suppose that either God has a weakness and cannot do the impossible or that God isn't good and won't do the impossible for you. Yet and still, God is so gracious to speak what is true over us, primarily about Himself. Renewing our minds in how we see Him and eventually ourselves.

What He spoke to Abraham, He says to us: *Is anything too hard for the LORD?* God is not like anyone you have or will ever know. He has no limitations. He is the one that made the heavens and the earth. He is the one who has all power. He is completely sovereign. Always strong and never tired. I'm positive that there is something in your life where this truth needs to be applied. It may be the salvation of a family member, the restoration of a marriage, deliverance from addiction, the opening of a barren womb, the resources to adopt, the power to forgive, the ability to put to death your favorite sins. Whatever it is, God can do it. Which isn't to say that everything you ask of God, He is obligated to do. God is God, and He has the right to move however and whenever He pleases. But the challenge is this: to believe that God is God. Which means, God can answer my impossible prayers, and the God of impossibility can give me an impossible faith to still trust Him if He doesn't.

Is there anything too hard for the Lord?

Be sober-minded; be watchful. Your adversary the devil
prowls around like a roaring lion, seeking someone
to devour. Resist him, firm in your faith, knowing that
the same kinds of suffering are being experienced by
your brotherhood throughout the world. 1 PETER 5:8-9

I'M NOT SAYING THE devil and demons are hiding under
every rock or lurking behind every corner, but they will put
their little greasy hands on whatever they can access. God
forbid you forget you have a real enemy actively working to
destroy you and everything you touch.

Paul told the church in Corinth to forgive an offender so that
they "would not be outwitted by Satan; for we are not ignorant of his designs" (2 Cor. 2:11). The motive to forgive was
an act of spiritual warfare. To withhold love would create an
opportunity for darkness to slip in between the cracks. Paul
was able to challenge the church because he wasn't naive
or resistant to the reality of the demonic and how it takes
advantage of everything. Paul wasn't "ignorant" to Satan's
schemes, but are you? When you are enticed and tempted
to covet or curse, do you *only* trace it to your flesh and not

also to the one who takes advantage of the weaknesses in your nature?

The world has been a bit vitriolic lately. It's easy to blame the intensity of politics and our natural bent toward tribalism, a perversion of true community, and not also remember how the devil is an enemy of peace. From what place does the thought "God doesn't love me" come? If lies were children, Satan is the father of them (John 8:44). When envy calls you by name and jealousy follows you home, do you ever consider its source? The Bible does: "If you have bitter jealousy and selfish ambition in your hearts . . . this is not the wisdom that comes down from above, but is earthly, unspiritual, demonic" (James 3:14–15).

Maybe, just maybe, we have become so rational that we've become unreasonable. Being ignorant to the devil's schemes is utterly unreasonable, and such ignorance is, in fact, one of his schemes. You won't resist an enemy you forget exists. You won't fight a devil you don't believe is real. After you open the blinds and let the light in, you will see that flesh and blood has never been the real enemy. There are rulers, authorities, "cosmic powers over this present darkness" and "spiritual forces of evil" with concentrated hate toward the people of God (Eph. 6:12). As creatures originally created by God, they are creative and thoughtful in the way they deal with you.

Your fight against evil, Christian, is one of resistance. Do that and the devil will flee (James 4:7). The power to resist, including the motivation, happens by faith. Faith in the same Jesus that "disarmed the rulers and authorities and put them to open shame, by triumphing over them in him" (Col. 2:15). Your faith is your weapon against the enemy of everything good. "In all circumstances take up the shield of faith, with which you can extinguish all the flaming darts of the evil one" (Eph. 6:16). And yes, resisting the evil one by faith can sometimes feel like putting on shoes not made for your feet and a war you don't have the stamina to win. But no worries. This cosmic conflict won't last always, for the God of peace is coming. The shoes you have on don't belong to you, but you will be victorious over the evil one as if they were. "The God of peace will soon crush Satan under *your* feet" (Rom. 16:20). Amen.

If there is among you anyone in need, a member
of your community in any of your towns within
the land that the LORD your God is giving you, do
not be hard-hearted or tight-fisted toward your
needy neighbor. You should rather open your
hand, willingly lending enough to meet the need,
whatever it may be. DEUTERONOMY 15:7-8 NRSV

IF EVER YOU DESPISE being needed—by people, children,
friends, spouses, ministry responsibilities or whatever—
remember God. On earth He was and in heaven He is always
needed by somebody. We need Him to "live and move and
have our being" (Acts 17:28). The activity of our lungs,
limbs, and life is dependent on God. As fruitful as we might
be in whatever mission we find ourselves commissioned to,
the growth belongs to someone transcendent of us.

The grace given to *do* is the same grace that was provided
for you to be. Both the being and the calling speak to an
innate need. Jesus said it this way: "Apart from me you can
do nothing" (John 15:5). As in, *no thing* can be done if Jesus
doesn't do it. The reasons we sometimes despise being needy
and needed are as diverse as an autumn sky. It would be

no surprise if somewhere beneath it all is an Adamic echo. The ground needed his hands. His hands needed Eve's help. After falling, they were still needy, but their perception of themselves, each other, and the world shifted, and thus, they lacked the wisdom and purity to discern their needs correctly.

A consequence of this is the impulse to live independently of one another, choosing self-sufficiency over community. We say things like, "I don't need nobody." So if ever somebody needs you, depending on your family of origin, you may be inclined to shame them for not idolizing independence as much as you do. We then refuse the call to cultivate and keep anything other than our own selves. And God forbid, somebody needs our love, our sacrifice, our time, our wisdom. It is then that our brother Cain resurrects in us saying, "Am I my brother's keeper?" (Gen. 4:9).

What's striking about Jesus's earthly ministry is not only His response to folks' constant needs but His inner disposition before meeting them. "And Jesus went throughout all the cities and villages, teaching in their synagogues and proclaiming the gospel of the kingdom and healing every disease and every affliction. When he saw the crowds, *he had compassion for them*, because they were harassed and helpless, like sheep without a shepherd" (Matt 9:35–36, emphasis added). People *needed* the good news, healing from various bodily diseases and afflictions, and knowing this, Jesus met them because He *cared*. The deepest parts of

Jesus's being, like a mother's love for her child, moved Jesus to meet folks where they were.

So a part of embracing the fact that you are needed, in whatever space you have been called, is identifying your own need for compassion. Once you receive it, then you can give it.

"Do you see anything?" And he looked up and said,
"I see people, but they look like trees, walking."
Then Jesus laid his hands on his eyes again;
and he opened his eyes, his sight was restored,
and he saw everything clearly. MARK 8:23-25

RIGHT BEFORE THIS, THE disciples were confronted by
Jesus about their lack of perception. They'd forgotten to bring
bread on their trip, to this place, and discussed the oversight
among themselves instead of resting in the One who was
on the boat with them. Jesus recognized their behavior as
springing up from the influence of unbelief (called leaven).
Testifying about Himself, He reminded them of how many
people He'd fed with very little and then asked, "Having
eyes do you not see?" (Mark 8:18).

Ironically, once the boat docks, a blind man is brought to
Jesus. Leaving the boat with those who see but don't see, He
encounters one for whom the issue of sight isn't a metaphor.
In what feels a bit odd to our cultural senses, Jesus puts
spit on the man's eyes and lays His hand on him too. Then
after asking the man if he could see, the man tells Jesus
that he can see people but they look like trees. Then the

text says, "Then Jesus laid his hands on his eyes again; and he opened his eyes, his sight was restored, and he saw everything clearly" (v. 25). The redundancy of the laying on of hands is not due to some insufficiency in Jesus. Let's not forget that through Him all things were made, and without him, nothing was made that was made (John 1:1–3).

The double healing isn't supposed to tempt us or trouble our hearts that maybe, just maybe, Jesus doesn't do all things well. This is a parable in action. The blind man represents the disciples who had eyes but could not see. They'd seen the miracles, heard the sermons, watched the divinity, but even still, people looked like trees and Jesus looked unclear. Their lack of understanding could only be overcome by grace, by Jesus's willingness and patience to heal and heal again until they could finally *see*.

Life has a blinding effect on the children of Adam. Or maybe a better way to say it is pride does. As it informs us, we can observe what's on the surface and completely miss what's beneath. It's the whole, "Set your mind on things that are above" principle (Col. 3:2). There is always more to see so long as you're dependent less on your own eyes, intellect, and wisdom and more on God's grace. If He doesn't finish the work, humble our hearts, reveal His glory, again and again and again, we will be completely satisfied with seeing trees instead of people. The world instead of heaven. Money instead of Jehovah Jireh. Our neighbor's offenses instead of the cross that handled them.

The Scriptures hold out to us the same question Jesus posed to the almost-blind man—"Do you see anything?" Answering the question Scripture asks of us will reveal how full or dim our sight might be so that by our confession God can deepen our spiritual depth and increase our understanding of His Son. We need Jesus to lay His hands on us again and again until that day when finally we shall see Him as He is.

[Jesus] told them, "It is not those who are well who need a doctor, but those who are sick. I didn't come to call the righteous, but sinners." MARK 2:17 CSB

DO YOU KNOW WHAT the difference was between the sinners sitting at the table and the sinners pointing their fingers at the table? It's that God had come to save both but only one side knew they needed Him.

Let me explain: "And Levi made him a great feast in his house, and there was a large company of tax collectors and others reclining at table with them. And the Pharisees and their scribes grumbled at his disciples, saying, 'Why do you eat and drink with tax collectors and sinners?' And Jesus answered them, 'Those who are well have no need of a physician, but those who are sick. I have not come to call the righteous but sinners to repentance'" (Luke 5:29–32). Jesus sitting with sinners. What a controversy and a mercy, if ever there was one. These people, blemished and unclean, sinful and unsanctified, would've dropped dead in the throne room, but on this night the Holy One sat and ate a meal with them.

The Pharisees and scribes were just as blemished as the "tax collectors and sinners" except they held positions and wore clothing that had a deceptive quality about it. An undiscerning eye would conclude that they, the teachers of the law and scribes of it, had to be holy too, right? Look at them, dressed like atonement. Present within the synagogue, schooled in the Scriptures, obedient to the Law, we'd surmise. But Jesus knew who and what they were even if no one else did. About them, He said, "You are like whitewashed tombs, which outwardly appear beautiful, but within are full of dead people's bones and all uncleanness" (Matt. 23:27).

Hypocrisy fools everybody but God. But the good news would've been fantastic if they believed the truth. The truth about the Law (including how they hadn't kept it), the Prophets, and the One sitting in front of them as a fulfillment of both. They believed they were healthy, but they had a sick mind. They thought they were clean when they needed to be cleansed.

In our day, there are plenty with the same spirit. They know Scripture, have family that do too—one that might've picked sins that don't sing as loud as the others. They got an ear for the spiritual, know the language of it by heart also, and they might be you. If ever you decided that anything you are or have done makes you good, you're deceived. And the deceived tend to think so highly of their own selves that they move toward death daily, full of pride and self-righteousness, while God stands with two nail-torn palms, waiting for them to come.

It's interesting that "obvious sinners" can be closer to the kingdom than the ones raised near it. Both the Pharisee and the tax collectors were under the same wrath. They both had the same fate, for the wages of all sin, secret and spoken, subtle and obvious, is death (Rom. 3:23).

But as God's grace would have it, Jesus was there, on earth, in the flesh, among sinners, so that they could be made right with His Father. Jesus didn't come for perfect people, for if He did, He would've only been coming for Himself. In love He was coming for the sick ones. They are and will always be the only ones who need Him, and they *know* it.

Then the man and his wife heard the sound of the
Lord God walking in the garden at the time of the
evening breeze, and they hid from the Lord God
among the trees of the garden. GENESIS 3:8 CSB

OUR FIRST PARENTS HID from God, and just like them, whose behavior we inherited, we do it too. For them it was when they heard God walking in the garden that they looked around, saw a tree, and made it a hiding place. When our hearts are hard on some level and the sound of God's voice comes through Scripture, or through the Spirit, or through a person He indwells, we always hide. The trees we find are as diverse as the sins that brought us there. If good works were an elm tree, we'd attempt to find safety in its shade. If ministry could be considered a pine tree, you'd find plenty of sinners behind it.

The good news is, no matter how far you go or how many mountains you climb, you cannot hide from God. The psalmist said: "Where can I go from your Spirit? Where can I flee from your presence? If I go up to the heavens, you are there; if I make my bed in the depths, you are there" (Ps. 139:7–8 NIV). Pride is the only reason anyone would believe God can't see them. Maybe it's because we've succeeded at hiding from everyone most of the time. And of course, there was that time when there was a knock on the door, the exposure of some hidden sin, the question that led to the confession you never wanted to make. But even those moments were orchestrated by the One who knew and made it known. He wanted it in the light, no matter how much it hurt, so you could be free. "Whoever conceals his transgressions will not prosper, but he who confesses and forsakes them will obtain mercy" (Prov. 28:13).

It's possible that hiding from people signals hiddenness before God. With Adam and the mother of all living, the tree became more than a reason not to confess. It was also an insufficient mediator. They knew the warning: "The day that you eat of it you shall surely die" (Gen. 2:17). And they supposed that a tree, a fellow creature, could protect them from judgment. They treated the tree like it was blood on the doorpost, like death would see the tree and pass over them.

Oh, how far we haven't fallen from the tree. We still invent ways of dealing with sin, hiding behind this or that as protection from the wrath of God. The conscience testifies to the truth, and like a hand over an honest mouth, we suppress it by any means necessary. But here it is again, for those with an ear to hear: salvation has not come via a created Savior. A created thing is an insufficient messiah. The only One that can make us right with God is God. The God who became a curse on a tree so that all who trust in Him can be forgiven (Gal. 3:13). He made a promise that a tree could never keep. And so, instead of hiding behind whatever your choice tree is, choose to tell God what brought you there in the first place. For "if we confess our sins, he is faithful and just to forgive us our sins and to cleanse us from all unrighteousness" (1 John 1:9).

God out. Tear them down with the truth about Christ, by the Spirit, as revealed in the Scriptures. Every brick has to go so that the Christ, the King of glory, can come in.

But Lot's wife looked back as she was
following behind him, and she turned into
a pillar of salt. GENESIS 19:26 NLT

WHEN JESUS TELLS US to remember anything, our memories need to pay attention. "Remember Lot's wife," He said in Luke 17:32. And do you? The woman married to Abram's nephew. The one who lived where angels knocked and lust-breathing men assembled like a community of haunted houses. Those angels came to Lot on a merciful assignment. God's hand had been lifted on the city, and judgment was a day away. Abraham had interceded, and in response God sent His ang ls to warn and rescue the prayed-for and judge the condemned. The door of salvation was opened to Lot and his entire family. His sons-in-law refused it, and Lot was slow to believe it. But mercy is also repetitive, so grabbing Lot, his two daughters, and his wife by the hand (remember her?), the angels snatched them out of the city and toward freedom.

As they left, the angels warned them again, saying, "Escape for your life. Do not look back or stop anywhere in the valley" (Gen. 19:17). Simple as the warning was, it must not have been easy to obey. From the sky came burning things sent from heaven like a gavel on fire. Their condemnation was just in fact; it's what they'd chosen. What is the rejection of God if not the acceptance of death? What is a longing glance toward Egypt if not proof of where your heart and citizenship really lie?

As or after the judgment on the city took place, Lot's wife (remember her?) looked back. And the text says she became a pillar of salt. The irony of it is plain. Refusing the life offered, she wanted the "life" she had. In nothing short of poetic justice, salt, a common preservative, embalmed the woman who wanted to preserve her life. By trying to save it, she lost it, becoming a monument of unbelief. A memorable one at that.

By remembering Lot's wife, we are reminded of a few things: (1) It's possible to get to the edge of deliverance and still miss it. Lot's wife left *with* Lot, her hands held by the angels on the way out. Leaving the city, she'd escaped judgment; and looking back, she immediately came under a different judgment by the same God. (2) Presuming upon mercy is a dangerous game to play. Perhaps Lot's wife recalled the angels coming to their home (a mercy), warning them of the coming judgment (a mercy), their urgency to rescue despite Lot's resistance (a mercy) and thought that just maybe she could do what shouldn't be done and mercy would meet her *again*. (3) Jesus told us, "Remember Lot's wife. Whoever seeks to preserve his life will lose it, but whoever loses his life will keep it" (Luke 17:32–33).

As each has received a gift, use it to serve one
another, as good stewards of God's varied grace:
whoever speaks, as one who speaks oracles of God;
whoever serves, as one who serves by the strength
that God supplies—in order that in everything God may
be glorified through Jesus Christ. To him belong glory
and dominion forever and ever. Amen. 1 PETER 4:10-11

EVERY CHRISTIAN HAS BEEN graced with some gift. There
are those who have been given the grace to open the Bible,
discern what the Spirit is saying throughout, and explain
it to God's people for their edification. Others have been
graced with mercy. They see the oppressed, the broken, the
needy and carry within them the God-given ability to also
see the image bearer beneath it all. Fighting for them instead
of against. Lifting them up and into freedom, in both soul
and body. Leaders are among the gifted too. Possessing that
heaven-empowered ability to see where people need to go
and what infrastructures need to be built. Casting vision and
washing feet.

When everyone functions in the grace they've received,
the body, a metaphor for the church, can walk on water.

Every woman, man, and child whom Christ has redeemed is equipped so as to "attain to the unity of the faith and of the knowledge of the Son of God, to mature manhood, to the measure of the stature of the fullness of Christ" (Eph. 4:13). That's the end goal for every gift given to men. To grow up in Jesus.

What do you think is an enemy of that aim? What holds the church back from fully being the tabernacle God designed it to be? It's the way we *think* about ourselves. Every gift has a thorn. The one gifted to teach pours out insight, and it doesn't take long before the *gift* and the *grace* to teach are attributed to the intellectual ability and personality of the teacher. Removed from their psyche is any consideration that what they were able to give, they first received. The merciful saint begins to think mercy is a part of their own nature, and so a diabolical pride develops in him, invisible to the eye of everyone but the Lord. They are thus tempted to test God, as Ananias and Sapphira did. Giving only as a means of honoring themselves. Using benevolence as a cover for selfish ambition.

Be a member of any church or Christian organization, and it won't be long before the thorns of a leader scar everyone he or she touches. The grace to lead lives alongside the temptation to control. To deify oneself, making the members of Christ's body the servants of an inflated ego and fragile estimation of their own worth. How we think about ourselves in light of our gifts will determine how and what we use them for. Either our glory or the Lord's.

The wisdom of the Spirit, working through Paul in his letter to Rome is for us too: "For by the grace given to me I say to everyone among you *not to think of himself more highly than he ought to think, but to think with sober judgment,* each according to the measure of faith that God has assigned" (Rom. 12:3, emphasis added). Modesty is often associated with clothing, but it's also appropriate for the mind. When we think about the particular gift we've received, like a balloon inflated and ready to fly, we must grab our thoughts by the hand and bring them back to earth. A drunken man cannot control his speech, or anything for that matter, but a sober man can think and see clearly, keeping himself and others safe. A sober mind works in the same way. It shields the gifted ones from seeing themselves in a light that transcends reality, and it guards the body from being unnecessarily wounded. The beginning of sobriety starts with the answer to this question: "What do you have that you did not receive?" (1 Cor. 4:7).

Now they had forgotten to bring bread, and they
had only one loaf with them in the boat. And he
cautioned them, saying, "Watch out; beware of the
leaven of the Pharisees and the leaven of Herod."
And they began discussing with one another
the fact that they had no bread. MARK 8:14-16

THERE'S A QUOTE THAT hasn't left my mind since reading
it. It goes: "The hardened heart is a particular problem for
religious and moral people (e.g., Rom. 2:5). An ignorant
heart cannot harden itself. Only a knowing heart can harden
itself, and that is why those closest to Jesus—the Pharisees
([Mark] 3:5–6) and the disciples (6:52; 8:17)—stand in the
gravest danger."[7]

This commentator is responding to a narrative in Mark 8.
Jesus has just fed four thousand people with seven loaves
of bread and rejected the Pharisee's demand for a sign from
heaven, as if the divine multiplication of bread wasn't good
enough. After both moments, we're invited into the boat with
the disciples and let into the tension of the text, which is
that the disciples have forgotten to bring enough bread for
their trip to Bethsaida.

Multiple men and one loaf, a miniature version of the situation they just experienced. Jesus perceives what's brewing in and between them, and He knows it's not their forgetfulness that's problematic but their perception. Before they say a thing, Jesus calls it out by saying: "Watch out; beware of the leaven of the Pharisees and the leaven of Herod" (Mark 8:15). The leaven of unbelief, an antagonistic posture toward Jesus by virtue of one's unwillingness to trust Him, has a home not only in the heart of the religious elite or political powers but also among the disciples. They are aware that they have forgotten bread. They want and need to eat to sustain themselves for the journey ahead, and yet they feel shame where Jesus hasn't chosen to condemn. As we all do at times, bullying ourselves for being weak instead of seeing it as an opportunity to trust Someone outside of ourselves.

To put it plainly, the disciples are in a boat with a man that fed five thousand people with five loaves of bread and four thousand people with seven loaves of bread—with some left over, mind you—and yet these men (who are significantly fewer than five thousand) default to talking about *what* they don't have before considering *who* they do have. To this, Jesus asks, "Why are you discussing the fact that you have no bread? Do you not yet perceive or understand? Are your hearts hardened? Having eyes do you not see, and having ears do you not hear? And do you not remember?" (vv. 17–18).

To those of faith, who have observed the Lord's hand, we have seen too much. We have watched Him provide for our needs. We have heard Him speak to us, through His Word, through His people, through His Spirit's presence in our heart, leading, guiding, warning, and comforting. We have experienced His peace and His deliverance. The most dramatic of it being that time He took out our heart of stone and gave us a heart of flesh. Or when He told us to "live," and we walked out of the grace and into new life.

May we resist the temptation to have eyes that don't see and ears that don't hear. To walk opposite of what has been revealed and affirmed as true, is to put stone back over an enfleshed heart. We who are near to Jesus are at risk of being hardened the most, seeing that we have seen His glory over and over again. The good news is that the One who revealed His glory is the One who will help us understand it too. Beware of the leaven of the Pharisees.

So then, there remains a Sabbath rest for the people of God, for whoever has entered God's rest has also rested from his works as God did from his. Let us therefore strive to enter that rest, so that no one may fall. HEBREWS 4:9-11

WHY IS REST SO hard? It could be that rest imposes certain limitations on us, putting us in the position to find purpose independent of our work. It feels validating to cultivate a thing. To till the soil, plant the seed, water the root, and watch it grow. We find joy in being able to step back and call a thing we've created "good." We were indeed called to this. On the seventh day, God rested. In the Law, He commanded it: "Remember the Sabbath day by keeping it holy" (Exod. 20:8 NIV). In Christ, He has become our rest. Wherein, Sabbath rest is no longer restricted to a day but experienced in a person.

There is a practical implication to this rest that modern readers would do well in pursuing. In which we cease from working, literally. Working for God's approval or working at all (where possible, for short or sustained period of times). The call to rest is in submission to the ultimate One, which is to love the Lord our God with all of our heart, mind, and soul. And truth be told, work has a way of disordering our affections and meddling with our mind, so much so that we begin to think we made the soil we tilled, found the seed we planted, created the water we used, and therefore the growth we called good is to our glory. Tim Keller put it this way:

> We are also to think of Sabbath as an act of trust. God appointed the Sabbath to remind us that he is working and resting. To practice Sabbath is a disciplined and faithful way to remember that you are not the one who keeps the world running, who provides for your family, not even the one who keeps your work projects moving forward.[8]

The rest we resist is for our good. It's a way to steward our entire selves. To sit down and just *think*. Or pray. Or meditate on grace and how it shows up in all the goodness we experience daily. Rest reorients us. Pausing makes room for memories. In silence and solitude, we can remember that man doesn't live by bread alone. In the cessation from work, whether five minutes or five days, we can recall that the manna came without Israel's help. In this rest, we can discover that God's provision isn't dependent on our hustle but on His goodness. Rest is indeed worship.

See, we count as blessed those who
have endured. JAMES 5:11 CSB

DID YOU KNOW THAT obedience comes with a cost? This isn't news to anyone who's looked upon the lives of the faithful. One group in particular, listed in Hebrews, describes both the cost of obedience and the person that helps us continue in it.

There is Noah who was told by God that He was about to destroy everything except his family. Meanwhile, everyone everywhere had a different conviction. To them, God's justice was a million miles away from their consciousness. They were busy with life and the ease that comes with a seared conscience. They were eating and drinking and getting married. Noah, however, didn't have the same luxury as the world around him. He was busy working to save his life. You don't think it took endurance for him to believe that God was telling the truth, especially when it seemed like nobody but him was concerned with God's judgment? You don't think he saw the relaxed nature of everybody else's life and coveted it sometimes?

Or consider Moses, the deliverer of God's people. Hebrews describes him as having "forsook Egypt" (Heb. 11:27 KJV). This means he turned his heart's affections away from the nation and its way of life. There is a cost to forsaking the kingdom of this world knowing that there is wrath for anyone who would dare say that Jesus is not only Lord of my heart but Lord of everything, everywhere.

There is a cost for the faithful ones. But do you know what makes one embrace it? Do you know what helped these saints keep going? Every single one of them didn't allow the cost of their obedience to distract them from the God they were obeying. Noah obeyed because he feared God (Heb. 11:7). And Moses endured by seeing the invisible God (11:27). And in the way of wisdom, we must do the same. Looking to Jesus, the eternal God, wrapped in flesh, crucified for sin, raised to life, and seated at the right hand of God must have our fear and our focus. As long as He does, every cost will be worth it.

Then they believed his words; they sang his praise. But they soon forgot his works; they did not wait for his counsel. But they had a wanton craving in the wilderness, and put God to the test in the desert. PSALM 106:12-14

ISRAEL COMPLAINED JUST AS much as we do. About any and everything. Adam's children are good at being specific. At identifying a problem and praising it by repeating its name. These complaints are often visceral—as in, they arise from something tangible and felt—rather than an abstract thing. Such as when Israel left Egypt, they grumbled against Moses and his brother by saying, "Would that we had died by the hand of the LORD in the land of Egypt, when we sat by the meat pots and ate bread to the full" (Exod. 16:3).

I can actually understand the angst. Hunger is an irritating feeling that tempts you to behave as if you've never eaten anything ever. What's problematic, though, is how if we let it have its way, the body will provoke us into missing a place we weren't even happy in. Let's not forget how Israel's time in Egypt was described. Taskmasters were set over them to "afflict them with heavy burdens" and "they ruthlessly made the people of Israel work as slaves and made their lives bitter with hard service, in mortar and brick, and in all kinds of work in the field. In all their work they ruthlessly made them work as slaves" (Exod. 1:11–14). Their bodies and the hunger within changed the way they thought about their previous condition. According to Israel, slavery wasn't bitter but bountiful. They ate as much as they wanted, when they wanted, they reason. They might've been slaves, but at least they had a full belly.

Oh, how the flesh makes heaven seem like hell and service to God seem more cumbersome than slavery to sin. At some point during any day, you'll see an attractive face (or whatever temptation finds you out), and you'll feel a pull toward it. That pull can linger if not resisted, and there are times when having to put something to death *is* the irritation. It *seemed* like in Egypt—when the world, the flesh, and the devil was Pharoah—when you were hungry, you ate. When you were thirsty, you drank. But what would've been at the end of it? Yes, you were "free" to do as you pleased, but once the full belly lived within a dead body, would the judgment seat of God have been worth the meal? The apostle Paul told the church in Rome the same: "For when you were slaves of sin, you were free with regard to righteousness. So what fruit was produced then from the things you are now ashamed of? The outcome of those things is death" (Rom. 6:20–21 CSB).

But you know the truth about those former days as well as I do. You were both a slave to a system and yourself back then. And now you've found a new Master, a good one, whose yoke is easy and burden is light. A King who is preeminent over all rulers and kingdoms. Revealing Himself as gentle and lowly. And life with that God is always better than life in Egypt.

This Lord has rescued the called ones and leads them into a wilderness of sorts where they will be hungry and they will thirst. And when they do, they must remember the truth about their previous position. That even when they ate, they were never full. Even if they drank, they were never free. And now, in this new land, there is bread from heaven and water from a rock. In Jesus, our bellies are full, and our thirst is quenched.

Who can fathom the Spirit of the LORD, or instruct
the LORD as his counselor? Whom did the LORD
consult to enlighten him? ISAIAH 40:13-14 NIV

WHENEVER GOD POSES A question at anyone in Scripture, I sit up straight and pay attention. For a God that knows all things to ask anyone anything, it must mean He is not simply being curious. The curiosity of God must be framed by the doctrine of omniscience. Job came to know it: "Will any teach God knowledge, seeing that he judges those who are on high?" (Job 21:22). And Paul appealed to it: "Who has known the mind of the Lord? Or who has been his counselor?" (Rom. 11:34 NIV). If God doesn't need a teacher, additional knowledge, or a counselor outside of Himself, then with every question, there's another motive behind the asking. To say it another way, if God knows everything and needs nothing, the act of divine inquiry must benefit the one who is being questioned alone.

With that in mind, the first recorded question in history posed to the first man in history is an interesting one. One that reveals God. Coming after the bite that darkened the world, the Lord was heard, walking in the cool of the day.

Was this His regular practice? We don't know. What we can observe is that the people, once blameless, now guilty, "hid themselves from the presence of the LORD God among the trees of the garden" (Gen. 3:8). Despite this, the Lord calls to Adam. His first words to him since He'd given him what's good in Eve. What got them here, blemished behind a tree, was their response to a question. And now Adam, and not Eve, is questioned *too*.

"Where are you?" God asked (v 9).

Imagine that? God, Creator of heaven and earth, the One who numbers the stars and searches the heart—the One whose sight no creature is hidden from no matter how many trees or ministries or masks it may crouch behind (Heb. 4:13)— asked Adam where he was. You may think that perhaps God needed to know his location. That as He walked through the garden, He squinted His eyes, looking to the left and right, needing to see before knowing, or ask in order to understand. But again, the transcendent God doesn't need anybody but Himself to know everything about everything. So consider the question again. Remember that another way to ask, "Where are you?" is to say, "Why are you not near?" Or ,"Why is there distance between us when all there has ever been is love?" Or, "Where are you *in relation to Me*?"

This question goes straight to the heart of what sin disrupts. Intimacy with God. To answer honestly, Adam must tell on himself. He must remember the fruit he took, calling the bite by name. God's question to Adam was an invitation more than it was inquiry. From the beginning then, God has been making room for the confession of sin. Making room to give up the futility of hiding from Him. If He knows everything, that includes me. My heart and the sin it loves. My mind and the thoughts it entertains. My body and the way it's treated.

And so, what a mercy it is to be questioned by God. It is evidence of love. The all-knowing God wants us to know and be known. It is reasonable to assume then that today divine curiosity on behalf of the sinner is still at work. In our pulpits and pews. In what we call "conviction" or the lack thereof. God knows exactly where you are, but do you? He's asking not to know but to bring you near.

So we fix our eyes not on what is seen, but on what
is unseen, since what is seen is temporary, but
what is unseen is eternal. 2 CORINTHIANS 4:18 NIV

THE KING OF SYRIA sent an army to come for Elisha once.
Angered that this prophet knew his secrets, the king directed
his army to find Elisha and seize him. Once the sun was
gone, the army surrounded the city like a predator in a bush,
waiting to snatch prey from its home.

Early in the morning, Elisha's servant awoke and looked out.
All around the city were chariots and horses and men being
carried by them. Naturally, the servant was afraid and asked
Elisha, *"What shall we do?"* (2 Kings 6:1, emphasis added).
He was looking for a strategy, I suppose. Elisha responds,
not with a technique on how to fight back or where to hide
from the sent ones, but with the reassurance that all that the
servant sees is not all there is.

Elisha tells the servant: "Do not be afraid, for those who are
with us are more than those who are with them" (2 Kings
6:16). Elisha's response was rooted in an invisible reality.
He then asks God to unveil it for his servant. For the natural

man can't discern spiritual things unless the invisible God helps him see behind the veil. "O LORD, please open his eyes that he may see" (2 Kings 6:17). Elisha petitions the Lord of heaven's armies to give the seeing servant sight. God answers, and when He does, the servant looks and sees another army, with horses and chariots, enflamed and surrounding not a city but a person. The invisible reality was made visible. The blinds were opened. The doors flung wide like praise or a hug or a smile.

The text doesn't say it, but I wonder what seeing the truth unveiled did for the servant's heart. What he saw was in response to how he felt, and how he felt must've changed after what he saw. Knowing now who and what was on his side, I bet he stood upright again.

Regrettably, most of us move throughout our days like the servant. Naturally. Skedaddling through life as if everything we can see is all that there is. Ignoring the spiritual reality of everything, such as angels and demons. Or the fact we worship an incarnate God, who has made the invisible God known. There's the reality that the Spirit of God is on the earth, in the church, giving us power to do impossible things like love our neighbor or carry our cross. Forgetting this, I believe, is the reason we behave as if we belong to this world. Commenting online about stuff that doesn't matter. Gossiping in the name of God. Wasting our time with the flesh. Scrolling through things that don't sanctify. Praying without power.

Elisha's prayer must be our own: God, open our eyes. Perhaps then, we will move with immovable faith. Constantly courageous. Overwhelmingly loving and eternally minded. This indeed would bring heaven to earth, or should I say, it's been here. In part, and one day in full. We just don't see it.

For I consider that the sufferings of this present
time are not worth comparing with the glory
that is to be revealed to us. ROMANS 8:18

MILLIONS OF PEOPLE IN every city, in whatever country, on this planet know pain by heart. They have been hurt by somebody, somewhere, and to them I say, use it. Use the pain. Pain has value in so far as we recognize its redemptive qualities.

There is Joseph of Genesis who was rejected, slandered, oppressed, and forgotten by people and yet seen by God. He was exalted as a lesser pharaoh, and by virtue of everything bad that he endured, he was able to save an entire nation.

There is Hannah's own body that refused to obey its design. Year after year after year, this woman was infertile and pro-voked by the other woman in her home because of it. This pain drove her into a temple, where she begged the Lord of hosts to give her a son with the vow that she would give him right back. God looked upon her affliction and remembered her prayer, giving her Samuel, a prophet and a priest who led God's people in truth.

There is David, a shepherd and a king who was haunted by the man he tried to serve and by the son who wanted his position. And in the midst of the fear and betrayal, do you know what he did? He wrote songs to God and for God's people. These songs were written in caves and in darkness, and yet they are Scripture. In the middle of trauma, David's words were breathed out by God, and till this day we all benefit from what he was able to create when he was hurting the most.

Then of course, there is Jesus our Lord. God of heaven, Creator of everything, Man of Sorrows. The King who bore "our griefs and carried our sorrows" (Isa. 53:4). The Almighty who was "despised and rejected by men" (Isa. 53:3). The Holy One who was "pierced for our transgressions" and "crushed for our iniquities" (Isa. 53:5). The purpose of the pain you ask? His wounds healed us. His punishment brought us peace. What greater example is there for how redemptive pain can be.

Even now, each abiding branch creates a garden of grapes, a vineyard of glory, only as the vinedresser prunes. God's ability to redeem what hurts will be realized one day, when we all see the eternal weight of glory that all of these light and momentary afflictions have been preparing us for (2 Cor. 4:17). So then, you hurt and hurting one, on this side of heaven, wherever there is pain, use it.

I will remember the deeds of the LORD;

yes, I will remember your wonders of old.

I will ponder all your work,

and meditate on your mighty deeds. PSALM 77:11-12

IN 1953, A MAN by the name of Henry Molaison went in for a brain surgery to treat his epilepsy. During the procedure, the doctor removed a piece of Henry's brain that affected his memory. Especially his short-term memory.

In one recording, a doctor doing a study on the brain and memory asked Henry if he remembered what he did yesterday. Henry responded with, "I don't know." The doctor asked another question. "Do you remember what you did this morning?" "I don't remember that either," Henry said. Then he was asked if he knew what he'd do tomorrow, to which Henry responded, "Whatever is beneficial."[9]

You'd expect him to have a loose schedule of some sort. That he'd at least say he'd wake up and get coffee. Call his mother, walk his dog. But Henry couldn't tell you what he'd do tomorrow because he couldn't remember what he did yesterday. He answered the questions the way he did because the portion of Henry's brain that was removed affected Henry's ability to make new memories, and since Henry couldn't remember the past, he had no context for how to imagine his future. Without his memories, Henry had no expectations.

When folks like Abraham thought about the sacrifice he had to make in the future, he remembered the resurrection in the past. He remembered how God gave him, a ninety-nine-year-old man, and his wife, a ninety-year-old woman, the power to conceive a son. Which was, in the truest sense, a kind of resurrection—life from dying bodies. Abraham's memories gave him context for his imagination. Therefore, if God could do a miracle then, then God could do a miracle now. That is *faith*.

Almost all of us have a hard time trusting God to do what He said He'd do, in His Word, through His Son, and it might be because we have a memory problem. How quickly we forget that He made the heavens and the earth, that He split the sea and delivered His people out of bondage, and how He brought life from a dead womb.

And beyond the biblical stories that happened ages ago, we forget how faithful He's been to us, our families, in our own lives in real time. How He provided for us when we didn't even ask. How He protected us from all kinds of mess. And so, when a trial shows up, we become like Henry, unable to recall the past, and because of it, we have no expectation for the future.

The truth is, the immutable nature of God is an anchor. It means that at no point in history or at no point in the time to come will God not be good. Or not able to move. He has and will always be a faithful and just and gracious and powerful God. Just because we change our minds every other minute doesn't mean God does. He is the same God today as He was then.

And so, I reckon that the spiritual discipline we'd all do well to cultivate is that discipline of remembering. And isn't that what the Word of God is for? To give us sixty-six books worth of memories about who God is and how God works? Which will inform our faith, so that we can always trust the Lord, without hesitation.

[Jesus] committed no sin, neither was
deceit found in his mouth. 1 PETER 2:22

A LOT HAS BEEN said about Jesus in the Scriptures, about how He used His words. As a boy, Jesus was found by His parents in the temple, sitting among the teachers, listening and asking questions. The text says that all who heard Him were astounded at His understanding and *His answers*. Jesus used wise words.

When driven into the wilderness by the Spirit in Matthew 4, one of the temptations in particular was for Jesus to use His words to command stones to become bread. The issue being that Jesus was being tempted to use His divine power to serve Himself. Jesus responded to each of Satan's temptations with the Scriptures. Jesus used God's words.

When a man, possessed by a demon, came out of a synagogue, Jesus spoke directly to the demon, commanded it to come out, to which the spirit obeyed. The onlookers said among themselves "What is this *word*? For with authority and power he commands the unclean spirits, and they come out!" (Luke 4:36). Jesus used liberating words.

One day while Jesus was asleep inside a boat, the wind and the waves started to break against it, filling the boat with water. While the disciples used their words to accuse Jesus of lacking a compassionate awareness of their needs, Jesus spoke directly to the sea saying, "Peace! Be still!" (Mark 4:39). Calming the wind. Calming the waves. Jesus spoke peacemaking words.

When a rich young ruler came to Jesus, asking how he could inherit eternal life. Jesus looked at the young man; He *loved* him and then *said* to him, "You lack one thing: go, sell all that you have and give to the poor, and you will have treasure in heaven; and come, follow me" (Mark 10:21). The rich young ruler walked away sad because he loved his money more than his Maker, and Jesus knew this. Jesus still spoke hard words.

That night in Luke 22 when Jesus was in a garden, kneeling on the ground, with sweat dripping from His face, the tangible awareness that soon and very soon He would carry a cross, and on it He would absorb God's wrath. This righteous wrath didn't belong to the Son because it was God's response to our sins. Not only the sins of the body but the sins of the tongue. Every harsh, hateful, racist, oppressive, unkind, lustful, manipulative, covetous, jealous, arrogant, self-righteous, and people-pleasing word we have or will ever speak necessitated the holy judgment of God. This holy rage was poured into a cup, and the Son knew that He came from heaven to earth for this moment. He knew that the cup was going to be poured out on Him. And in that moment, what did He do? He used His words to speak with His Father. "Father, if you are willing, remove this cup from me. Nevertheless, not my will, but yours, be done" (Luke 22:42). Jesus used obedient words.

And then, when on that cross, after our sins and their judgment were placed on the innocent Son of God, before giving up the ghost, Jesus spoke the words that saved your life: "It is finished" (John 19:30). Jesus used redemptive words.

Children of the living God, behold Jesus. In Him we see what it looks like to use our words in a way that shows God as glorious and honors the glory in the image bearers He has made.

Therefore, since we are surrounded by so great a cloud of witnesses, let us also lay aside every weight, and sin which clings so closely, and let us run with endurance the race that is set before us, *looking to Jesus*, the founder and perfecter of our faith, who for the joy that was set before him endured the cross, despising the shame, and is seated at the right hand of the throne of God. HEBREWS 12:1-2, EMPHASIS ADDED

AS YOU RUN THE same race as the writer of Hebrews, what helps you keep going? I hope the answer is Jesus. I don't know how long you've been running, but if you're doing it with your focus on anything else but the Christ, you're not going to finish this race.

A real spiritual attack, in the form of temptation, tells you that the way to endure sin is to sin. If there is sexual frustration in your marriage, instead of petition, some turn to porn so as to deal with the constant disappointment or rejection. Or we entertain inappropriate friendships as a way to cope with loneliness. Or it could be an addiction like alcoholism or even social media, which works as a numbing agent for our weary hearts. But as John said, I'll say to you: "Little children, keep yourselves from idols" (1 John 5:21). This race will never be easy, but the sin that clings and the weight that hinders must be laid aside because whether you realize it or not, it's making your race harder to run.

I fear that within the church, in today's era, a whole bunch of us have run without Jesus for so long that we aren't running at all. May God soften every hardened heart and every seared conscience. The only way to run well is to look at God often. How? We know this, don't we? But I'll remind you.

There's this book called the Bible. In it are sixty-six other books that all point to, describe, and explain God. In ministry it's typical that the Bible so quickly becomes a tool for us or a mere resource, but this thing is alive. It will speak to you a new thing with the same words. Read to see His goodness, His kindness, His faithfulness, His beauty. Read to remember what He thinks about you and the world. Read it to remind yourself what has come before us and what will come after. Read it to see the life, death, and resurrection of Christ.

But not only that; you must actually believe what it says. We have enough people in the church that are well equipped to handle a passage exegetically with no evidence of them living it historically. We must believe the Bible. We must believe what God has said about Himself as revealed in His Son. And as we continue to hold fast to it, we will finish our race because of it.

God said, "I will make my dwelling among them
and walk among them, and I will be their God, and
they shall be my people." 2 CORINTHIANS 6:16

WHEN ALL WAS WELL with God and man, there was perfect
unity. Closeness. Perhaps God deciding to walk through the
garden, in the cool of the day, even after the invention of sin,
speaks to this curious intimacy. Soon after, because God is a
Holy One and Adam was no longer, "the LORD God sent him
out from the garden of Eden," and "He drove out the man"
(Gen. 3:23–24). Distance.

Generations go by, and this dynamic of the Holy God at arm's
length with men is evident when the Lord calls to Moses out
of the bush, and immediately Moses is warned, "Do not come
near" (Exod. 3:5). God reveals Himself as the God of Israel's
patriarchs, and Moses hides since "he was afraid to look at
God" (v. 6). At another time, Moses asks to see God's glory.
God offers His back and not His face *for man shall not see
me and live"* (Exod. 33:20, emphasis added). Distance.

On that great mountain, when God came to make covenant
with a sinful people, He warned again, "Go down and warn

the people, lest they break through to the LORD to look and many of them perish" (Exod. 19:21). Distance.

Remember Uzzah. Carrying the ark precariously, the oxen stumbled, and Uzzah reached out His hand to touch the ark. "And the anger of the LORD was kindled against Uzzah, and God struck him down there because of his error" (2 Sam. 6:7). Distance.

Story after story. Book after book. Between Genesis and Malachi is the testimony of God's people, unable to see and touch God without the threat and exercise of judgment. Sin is so unnatural, so unlike the King of glory that it creates distance between God and man. By both choice and command.

Until we get to Luke 2. Concerning Mary, the text says, "The time came for the baby to be born, and she gave birth to her firstborn, a son. *She wrapped him in cloths and placed him in a manger*" (vv. 6–7 NIV, emphasis added). Concerning the shepherds, the text says, "So they hurried off and found Mary and Joseph, and the baby, who was lying in the manger. When they had *seen him*, they spread the word concerning what had been told them about this child" (vv. 16–17 NIV, emphasis added).

Understand the weight of this. For Jesus to be swaddled, God had to be *touched.* The shepherds spread the word about the God they'd *seen.* The Word that was God had become flesh and dwelt among them (John 1:14). No wonder Matthew lifted up the words of Isaiah when he said, "'Behold, the virgin shall conceive and bear a son, and they shall call his name Immanuel' (which means, God with us)" (Matt. 1:23). Imagine that? The Holy God drawing near to us. The Holy God dwelling with us. A kindness and a mercy in one.

The apostles said to the Lord, "Increase our faith!" And the Lord said, "If you had faith like a grain of mustard seed, you could say to this mulberry tree, 'Be uprooted and planted in the sea,' and it would obey you." LUKE 17:5-6

CONSIDER THAT FAITH CAN move mountains and devils. We know faith is a resource in many respects. By grace, through it, we've been reconciled to God. We reckon it useful when casting cares and making petitions. The writer of Hebrews ran out of time when trying to explain the power faith effects. And how because of it, the saints of old "conquered kingdoms, enforced justice, obtained promises, stopped the mouths of lions, quenched the power of fire, escaped the edge of the sword, were made strong out of weakness, became mighty in war, put foreign armies to flight" (Heb. 11:33–34).

But like I said in the beginning of all of this, faith can move mountains and devils. Faith is a form of resistance against the evil one. We can sing to the top of our lungs about stepping on the devil's head, but if we have no faith, our fight will be all words and no power. The apostle Paul speaks of faith as a part of spiritual warfare by saying, "In all circumstances take up the shield of faith, with which you can extinguish all the flaming darts of the evil one" (Eph. 6:16). Having armor with no shield is ridiculous in every way. The entire body is a billboard for death. Welcoming it by its lack of protection.

Devils have a million fiery missiles to throw, all aiming for one thing: your faith. They aren't primarily concerned with a marriage or even a ministry, with a person's income or intellect; they will throw a dart at each only as a means of getting at the faith that influences each sphere. Each dart, when thrown, poses a challenge at the soldier's framework for God. Is He good? Or near? Does He see me? Love me? Like me, even? Will God come through? Will He deliver? Is the Scripture authoritative? Where there is no faith, the darts land and burn everything down. Where there is no faith, God isn't pleased. For what other thing would Satan take joy in than a church full of people who sing about a God they don't believe? And preach from a text they don't honor? Maybe, just maybe, the real reason for the godlessness of this nation is that we have too many soldiers with no shields—too many believers with no faith.

The good news is that the shield of faith wasn't earned but received. It's a gift from a King. So even if you've put it down for a moment or for a season, only a mustard seed of faith is required for you to pick it up again. The Founder and Perfecter of your faith is worthy to be trusted and believed and relied on. Believe Him and every arrow must fall. Every fiery dart from the evil one will be quenched by the shield of faith because faith will move mountains and devils.

"Father, if you are willing, remove this cup from me. Nevertheless, not my will, but yours, be done." LUKE 22:42

IT'S ONE THING TO know that God is able and another to know if He is willing. I say this after reading about the three Hebrews boys in Daniel 3. Defying Nebuchadnezzar's order to worship the silly image he set up, Nebuchadnezzar confronted them with the threat of a burning furnace. If they chose by some foreign insolence to remain standing when everyone else bowed and silent when everybody else praised, the judgment for it would be bodies made into ashes. Their bodies, that is.

These boys with these bodies were known by an image no man can see and live. They'd inherited stories told and remembered about this God, their God, Yahweh. In exile, they probably rehearsed what was told about His presence in the bush, the making known of His name, and the eventual deliverance of His people with many signs and wonders. Then came the covenant and the wilderness, the rebellion and the exile, but God, their God, hadn't changed one bit.

With that kind of history with God, why would they be concerned with a narcissistic king and a fiery furnace? God, their God, had overcome political powers and elements before. So He was more than able to do it again, but was He willing? In response to the threat thrown in their direction, they stood ten toes down and said, "If this be so, our God whom we serve is able to deliver us from the burning fiery furnace, and he will deliver us out of your hand, O king. But if not, be it known to you, O king, that we will not serve your gods or worship the golden image that you have set up" (Dan. 3:17–18). They had faith in two directions, faith in God's power, as in, His ability to deliver. And faith in God's freedom to choose, for them, deliverance or death.

Contentment with the latter is the test for many. We can count on millions of hands all of the hard hearts made by God's will not being their own. We know He can heal, but if He doesn't, will you still worship? We know He can bless in a diversity of ways, but when He picks the blessing that hurts instead, will you still love Him?

It's a hard pill to swallow, I know, but Jesus drank the cup dry. He too, trusted the Father in two directions. Though He knew that with one call to heaven, twelve legions of angels would come to His aid. God was able to take the cup away, and Jesus, more than anyone, knew the might of El Shaddai. Yet and still, He said what we'd do well to repeat: "Nevertheless, not my will, but yours, be done" (Luke 22:42).

See, we have left everything and
followed you. MATTHEW 19:27

GOD IS GOOD AT all things, especially the art of interruption. He interrupted Paul's journey and Jacob's walk. He interrupted Nebuchadnezzar's pride and Abraham's almost-sacrifice. God became flesh, dwelt among men, and continued as usual, to interrupt things. The early disciples experienced this, when on regular, uneventful days, Jesus came into their lives and made them into some other thing. And not into something that wasn't life but something that was life as it should've been. A life with Him in it.

For the disciples, the interruption happened with words, only two of them:

"Follow me."

I've always wondered what the tone of it would've been. Without hearing the sound, I don't know if it was urgent or calm, assertive or something else. What I do know is it wasn't a suggestion or a request but a command. Sort of like, "Lazarus, come out." And "let there be light."

When God speaks, things move, including people. At the sound of it, Simon and Andrew "immediately they left their nets and followed him" (Matt. 4:20). And for Zebedee and John, immediately they left the boat and their father and followed him. Levi "got up, left everything and followed him" (Luke 5:28 NIV). Isn't it strange how Jesus's command didn't have additional instructions, but maybe by faith they knew what it required. Each one of them "left" something. Their nets, their boat, their father, *everything*. They left everything. Jesus said to them, eventually: "And everyone who has left houses or brothers or sisters or father or mother or children or lands, for my name's sake, will receive a hundredfold and will inherit eternal life" (Matt. 19:29).

With two words Jesus became King. Those words a summons. Their lives, as they knew it, were united into His. No wonder "follow me" is treated by the world and those who love it as if it were a curse. They hear it and think of all the sparkly things they'd have to leave behind. And they're right. Jesus is either Master or nothing. If at any point you believe "Jesus and some other thing" is a viable possibility, you've chosen the wide way. As King, He is worthy of our full allegiance, and as Savior, He's provided the way of escape (from sin and therefore lies) that prevent us from seeing the path of forsaking all as the journey of joy.

Paul discovered this for himself. After turning from the sparkly things, he saw how worthless they all were only when He compared what he left to the One he was leaving it all for. He said, "I count everything as loss because of the surpassing worth of knowing Christ Jesus my Lord" (Phil. 3:8). Side by side with Jesus, the world looks dimmer than we thought. Less interesting than how we praised it for being. But with Jesus, no matter who and what we put Him next to, His glory wins every time. So whatever your "everything" is, leave it and follow the King.

Do your best to present yourself to God as one
approved, a worker who has no need to be ashamed,
rightly handling the word of truth. 2 TIMOTHY 2:15

JAMES SAID A WISE albeit discouraging word when he suggested, "Not many of you should become teachers" (James 3:1). It would seem to me that, from the vantage point of any lover of the Scriptures, teaching would be a worthwhile pursuit. Opening the text in a pulpit or living room, discerning its meaning and applying it too, all function to "equip the saints for the work of ministry" and to "build up" the church (Eph. 4:12). The ability is a gift and a grace and, for some, a call.

So then, back to the beginning of this entire thing. If a teacher is good and necessary, graced and gifted, why shouldn't many people become one? The end of the verse answers: "Not many of you should become teachers, my brothers, for you know that we who teach will be judged with greater strictness" (James 3:1). It's possible that James has his eye on those within a congregation that are zealous to teach, not because they want to equip the saints but because they want the honor that comes with it. The teacher of Christian doctrine was, in one sense, the reimagining of the Jewish rabbi. The venerated elite, teachers of the law, explained glory and received it. To the detriment of their own souls sometimes, "for they loved the glory that comes from man more than the glory that comes from God" (John 12:43). A covetous congregant will create a strategy to receive glory, by means of mimicking a gift they don't have or by prostituting the ones they do.

I suspect that more now than ever, this hellish hustle is done with greater ease. Look around at all of the options, outside of a local congregation, which should have systems in place to train and/or withhold the practice of said gift. But with the Internet, all one needs to teach is a phone and a mouth. If it's easier now to become a "teacher" than it was then, then there are also more people that will stand before the Holy One and hear a judgment they weren't prepared for. If it isn't social media preachers, it's Bible study leaders, seminary professors, Sunday school teachers. Each space is constructed in such a way that somebody will be considered a teacher, and James wants the saints to know, *this may not be what you want.* Which isn't intended to make someone fearful; it's to make us reverent.

With that said, with whatever gift you've been graced, if a teacher, take seriously the warning of our Lord's brother. If something else, pray for the teachers you know and the ones that want to be known. In Jesus's name, Amen.

Have mercy on me, O God,
according to your steadfast love;
according to your abundant mercy
blot out my transgressions.
Wash me thoroughly from my iniquity,
and cleanse me from my sin!
. . . Against you, you only, have I sinned and
done what is evil in your sight.
. . . Behold, I was brought forth in iniquity,
and in sin did my mother conceive me.
. . . Create in me a clean heart, O God,
and renew a right spirit within me.
. . . The sacrifices of God are a broken spirit;
a broken and contrite heart, O God, you will
not despise. PSALM 51:1-2, 4, 5, 10, 17

AFTER HIS SIN WITH Bathsheba, David repented in song, as recorded in Psalm 51. One memorable lyric or verse, for which Fred Hammond put an organ behind, was his request for God to create in him a clean heart. After Nathan confronted David and the Spirit imbued him with contrition, David found refuge in the truth of who he was and what that meant. "Behold, I was brought forth in iniquity, and in sin did my mother conceive me" (v. 5).

There was a reason for David's behavior. The sin he was born in led him to see in Bathsheba merely a body and not an image bearer. To choose lust over legacy. To dishonor the Lord of hosts, who was able to give him victory on the roof (if only he asked) just as He gave him in the field with the sling and stones.

This kind of self-awareness encourages repentance. If the sin is, in fact, someone else's, then the guilty one isn't actually the guilty one. Like Adam, whose finger lifted toward God as if He were to blame for his faith in the devil, "The woman whom *you* gave to be with me, she gave me fruit of the tree, and I ate it" (Gen. 3:12, emphasis added). David understands, as the brokenhearted saint often does, that "good itself does not dwell in me, that is, in my sinful nature" (Rom. 7:18 NIV). His sin was his own, and it was endemic to his nature.

Now pay attention. This degree of confession and self-inspection is a sort of invitation for the serpent, the crafty one. Once he knows you know yourself, he will place in your mind the idea that who and what you are right now is how you will remain. What begins as healthy introspection turns into an inordinate preoccupation with self instead of the Son of God. The meditation of your heart centers on your failure and not Christ's faithfulness. Your weaknesses and not Christ's strength. The shame you feel becomes all you can see. And the by-product of worshipping shame is that it begets more sin. Simply because shame isn't your Savior. Jesus is.

If that's reality and it is, we must take heed to the exhortation of Hebrews that tells us to look, fix, keep our eyes on Jesus. Who, might I add, is the Creator of all things, including you. The you that was born and shaped in iniquity. The you that has nothing good in you. In his repentance, David asked God to do a miracle in him. If God were to create a new heart in David, David would be a new man. The depth of his self-awareness could've turned into self-absorbed shame, but it opened the door for God-oriented petition. David knew that if he was as sinful as he knew he was, then only God could make him who he needed to be. So then, our hope is not within us but before us, in Christ, who makes all things, including our hearts, new.

DAY 53

Let us hold fast the confession of our
hope without wavering, for he who
promised is faithful. HEBREWS 10:23

CYNICISM IS EASY. IT doesn't take effort to see what's wrong with everything and everyone and let it jade us. Hope, however, is difficult. Maybe because it's heavenly. The earth has worn on us some. Suggested to us, through things like abandonment and failed expectations that hope is no different from wishful thinking. But hope is more than that. As one helpful book explains, "Hope allows us to go on with living. It gives us some sense that things are going to get better. Life will improve, and the problems besieging us will reach some stage of resolution."[10]

Maybe even now, after reading that sentence, you smirked wide and willful, just like the skeptic the earth has made you. I'm confident this is why the apostle Paul not only recommended hope but prayed for the church to be filled with it. "May the God of hope fill you with all joy and peace in believing, so that by the power of the Holy Spirit you may abound in hope" (Rom. 15:13). See its source? The God of hope. Through what power? The Holy Spirit, who helps us abound in it.

At this point, I think it's wise to acknowledge spiritual warfare, even in discussions on hope. Only the devil, the hopeless one, would influence saints, redeemed of God, united with Christ, made alive by His Spirit, to believe *they* have no hope. That there's no abundant life to be lived. That things don't change or grow or transform. The hopeless would be realists insofar as the tomb wasn't empty. "And if Christ has not been raised, your faith is futile and you are still in your sins. Then those also who have fallen asleep in Christ have perished. If in Christ we have hope in this life only, we are of all people most to be pitied" (1 Cor. 15:17–19). If we lived here, with all of its woes and worries, and that was *it*. No golden streets and "holy, holy, holys." No glorified body in a city without lamps and plenty of light. No vengeance on the wicked, including the ones who injured our desires, trampled our expectations, making it hard to hope for anything good. If this was all there is, hope would be the language of fools.

Thankfully hope is not the language of fools, though. Thankfully it's the strength of the wise, so we refuse the evil one and the consideration of his lies. We do this by rejoicing in hope (Rom. 12:12), for by doing so, we believe that "hope does not put us to shame, because God's love has been poured into our hearts through the Holy Spirit" (Rom. 5:5). And our hope—in Christ, that is—is not wishful thinking; rather it strengthens the weak and makes eagles on the earth: "But those who hope in the LORD will renew their strength. They will soar on wings like eagles; they will run and not grow weary, they will walk and not be faint" (Isa. 40:31 NIV).

"I will fortify the house of Judah, and the house
of Joseph I will save. I will surely bring them back,
because I care about them. . . . Since I am the LORD
their God, I will answer them." ZECHARIAH 10:6 ISV

HAVE YOU EVER EXPERIENCED a circumstance God allowed you to endure that discouraged you to the point that it became natural for you to think the worst about God? That He's not good? That He doesn't care?

Those ideas and discouragements are nothing new. When the Serpent confronted Eve in the garden, he didn't just cast doubt on God's Word but also God's nature. He deceived her by saying she could eat from the tree because "God knows that when you eat of it . . . , you will be like God" (Gen. 3:5). As if God were holding Eve back from something good. When in reality, His restrictions were protection.

Or consider Christ. When Jesus was in the wilderness, fasting for forty days and forty nights, the devil came to Him and said, "If you are the Son of God, command these stones to become loaves of bread" (Matt. 4:3). If You are the Son of God, why are You hungry? Take advantage of Your divine power to feed Yourself since Your Father hasn't. The devil tried with Jesus the strategy he succeeded in with Eve, which was to tempt God's Son to distrust God's care.

And sometimes this accusing tone doesn't come directly from the devil's mouth. Sometimes it comes through those he has influenced and tempted, those who are walking according to his logic without knowing it. When the disciples were in a boat that was being bullied by the waves, Jesus was asleep at the bottom of it. They came and woke Him, not with petitions but with accusations saying, "Teacher, do you not care that we are perishing?" (Mark 4:38). Care? The whole reason He came to earth was because He cared. "For God so loved the world, that he gave his only Son, that whoever believes in him should not perish but have eternal life" (John 3:16). And He not only cares about your soul but also cares about your cares. All of the worries that keep you up at night. Through the pen of Peter, His Spirit said, "Cast your cares on Me, for I care about you" (1 Pet. 5:7, adapted). Not just love you, but care for you.

And that, my friend, is what the flesh and the devil, through discouragement, will tempt you to doubt. He would have you believe that the God who died for you doesn't actually care about you. And I exhort you in this way: the devil is a liar. If there is any being that doesn't care about you, it's him. But your Lord, your God, loves you with an everlasting love. He is "the LORD, the LORD, the compassionate and gracious God" (Exod. 34:6 NIV).

But you will receive power when the Holy
Spirit comes upon you. ACTS 1:8 NLT

BEFORE JESUS ASCENDED TO the Father, He promised
a helper (John 15:26). Not too long after, in one place, the
disciples were gathered. Then came a sound, like a violent
wind from heaven. Above them, what looked like tongues
of fire rested. As it happened, a filling did too. The Holy
Spirit manifested, sort of like Jesus said He does: "The wind
blows where it wishes, and you hear its sound, but you do
not know where it comes from or where it goes. So it is with
everyone who is born of the Spirit" (John 3:8).

After the filling, they didn't run or shout or even cry; they
began to speak. Out of each mouth came another tongue. As
the sentences flew out, the languages of nations not their
own took up space. The wonders of God had a sound, and a
diversity of ears heard it. There's no time to get caught up in
the doctrinal controversies that arise from texts like this. To
the point that our eyes glaze over, missing specific glories.
For example, James told us: "The tongue is a fire, a world
of unrighteousness. . . . For every kind of beast and bird, of
reptile and sea creature, can be tamed and has been tamed
by mankind, but no human being can tame the tongue. It

is a restless evil, full of deadly poison" (James 3:6–8). And yet here, in this room, with this gathering of people, we see the Holy Spirit taming what can't be tamed. A tongue of fire imparting heavenly life instead of earthly venom. Like a dog with a leash, a ship with a rudder, a horse with a bit, the tongue found its Master when the Holy Spirit filled the room.

A morning is on the way when you didn't rest like you wanted and get the energy you think you needed, and when that happens, the tongue becomes a match, the flesh the flame. Maybe it will be next week when a person, any person, will tempt you to forget heaven but swallow the flame and watch the smoke. Treat silence like a burnt offering. A soft answer as worship. Neither way is possible if the wind doesn't come.

The only way to control the uncontrollable is to be filled with a foreign Power. That is, the Holy Spirit. And when He comes into the room and the mouth opens, the sound of it is joyful and peaceful and patient and gentle and kind and good and self-controlled and loving. Everything the Spirit is, is everything the Spirit can empower us to speak.

But we have this treasure in jars of clay, to
show that the surpassing power belongs to
God and not to us. 2 CORINTHIANS 4:7

EVERY DAY OF OUR lives, something happens that reminds us of our fragility. Some of us open the day with too many burdens to count. Have you ever slept but didn't rest and awoke to a body that felt heavy laden? Ever been spoken to and about in a way God wouldn't like, all because you not only liked but loved His name? Once a person decides to make war on the kingdom of darkness, slaves of it rise up to defend it by any means necessary. This wears on us sometimes. It's that uncomfortable feeling of knowing somebody hates you for loving them.

Outside of the hostility we experience from those who are ultimately citizens of this world, so many other things expose our weaknesses and the limits of our humanity. Affliction is diverse. One day, death comes to somebody we loved and wanted to stay. Another day, the body starts to break, bit by bit, unglorified now but not forever. Then there's next week when the manna is all gone, the job lost, the economy crashes, the husband leaves, or the wife's mind wonders. If these trials happen all at once, we cry for deliverance from this place. And maybe we've done that already, and God said, "Not yet." Either way, earth ain't heaven and we know it.

But guess what? It ain't hell either. There's a greater glory, a shining light, a good King and wonderful Savior that saved us. He gave us power to trample over serpents and to deny the flesh. As we do, we still hurt some days. And on other days, we help heal the hurting. Isn't it something to have power and weakness in the same body? But that's how it all works.

The apostle said, "We are afflicted in every way, but not crushed; perplexed, but not driven to despair; persecuted, but not forsaken; struck down, but not destroyed; always carrying in the body the death of Jesus, so that the life of Jesus may also be manifested in our bodies" (2 Cor. 4:8–10). Jars of clay crack easily. But when they do, it means whatever is in it can be seen. Glory be to the all-powerful God that, even when we crack, we won't break.

If we are faithless, he remains faithful—for
he cannot deny himself. 2 TIMOTHY 2:13

AFTER MIRIAM WENT BACK to God in Numbers 20, the
people complained again. This time it was about water,
again. One of the early occasions when thirst turned their
faces away was just a few chapters before in Exodus 17.
Having no water, they made a fuss. So Moses cried out to
the God of this people, and God responded with the simple
command to *strike* the rock (v. 6). Once Moses did, water
came out and quenched a nation.

As if it were tradition for Israel to forget God when thirsty,
you'd expect Numbers 20 to turn out just like Exodus 17.
Two different stories with the same characters except when
this people complained, Moses didn't cry. A noteworthy
distinction, for it implies that Moses didn't plead. Didn't
summon the God of his heart to fill him first before satisfying
the others.

We forget the Moses we met in Egypt in Exodus 2—the Moses
who took matters into his own hands once and murdered a
man as if to mediate in the flesh (vv. 11–15). That "Exodus 2"
Moses was still in this "Exodus 17" one, but what kept him

at bay and all the rage he brought with him was prayer. Number the times in Scripture you read the words "cried out to the Lord" next to Moses's name, and the way this story ends will make all the sense in the world. Because when the people complained *this* time, the "Numbers 20" Moses may have fallen on his face before the Lord, but he didn't say a thing. God spoke first and told Moses, "Take the staff, and assemble the congregation, you and Aaron your brother, and *tell the rock* before their eyes to yield its water. So you shall bring water out of the rock for them and give drink to the congregation and their cattle" (Num. 20:8, emphasis added).

Moses takes the staff, gathers the people, and then for the first time in this narrative, Moses's speaks. And *not to the rock* but to the people: "Hear now, you rebels: shall we bring water for you out of this rock?" (v. 10). The words of a man who lay prostrate before God and yet got up without petitioning Him (v. 6). From this place of arrogant rage, Moses takes the staff and strikes the rock not once but twice. Anger is never abated easily.

Even though Moses doesn't do as God commanded, by striking instead of speaking, the water still comes in abundance. Which is to say that if God has determined to bless His people, the sins of the leader will not get in the way of God's grace. Which is also to say that there will be and most likely have been times when you have mimicked obedience. Took the staff, got near the rock, but struck it instead of speaking to it, and the water came anyway. This should remind you that if God has determined to bless His people, He will do it despite your disobedience. His mercy toward others has never been dependent on your perfection. God's people received the water not because of anything Moses did or didn't do but because God is faithful.

That's the beautiful part. God is faithful to satisfy the needs of sinful people. But make no mistake about it, He was also faithful to discipline the failure of their leaders. Paul's words are applicable: "But I discipline my body and keep it under control, lest after preaching to others I myself should be disqualified" (1 Cor. 9:27). God's faithfulness alone is the hope of the flock *and* the hope of the leader.

"But when you pray, go away by yourself,
shut the door behind you, and pray to your
Father in private." MATTHEW 6:6 NLT

PICK A GOSPEL, MAYBE Luke or Mark, read it through in one sitting, and make note of the pace of Jesus's life. From the second He turned water into another thing, He was busy. One moment He's loosing bodies of the demons within them. Another time, He's healing the sick of fevers, of leprosy, of blind eyes and dark hearts. In between and around these, Jesus preached. About Himself, as the anointed One. About the Father, as the One who sent Him. And mind you, none of the work was located in one city. He was in Nazareth, in Cana, in Caesarea Philippi, in Bethany, in Capernaum. Whenever He did a work in a new place, the travel was on foot. The traveling God eventually became known by many for all the beauty (and controversy) He brought into a place.

With all of that in mind, verses like these are striking: "But now even more the report about him went abroad, and great crowds gathered to hear him and to be healed of their infirmities. But he would withdraw to desolate places and pray" (Luke 5:15–16). Jesus would momentarily forsake the work to be with God.

If Jesus were on mission in our day, someone might've suggested that He do the opposite. They'd never encourage Him not to pray of course. That's obviously unchristian, right? But what they would do, as they do with anybody in Christian ministry, is place ministry demands, expectations, and pressures on Him in ways that inevitably served the work more than the intimacy needed to accomplish it.

How many of us are so busy in the name of Jesus, that we're forsaking Jesus? So burdened with organizing this, volunteering for that, writing this, teaching here, meeting with this friend, showing up to that event, changing this diaper, listening to that mentee that we don't even have the power or the joy to be like Jesus in all of our doing? And don't miss the text. It says "great crowds gathered to hear him and to be healed of their infirmities." Meaning, there were endless opportunities for the Christ to show up for people in ways they legitimately needed.

But He could not let the needs of the people have more influence over His time than intimacy with His Father. The Christ who told us to abide in Him, abided in the Father. The Christ who taught His disciples to pray, prayed to the Father. The Lord of the Sabbath literally rested in the Father. "One could make a strong case," one pastor writes, "that the fully human Jesus was able to live the life he did because of the constant time and energy put into being with the Father in prayer."[11]

God has called us to do much. It is a grace to be a laborer in a plentiful harvest, but there must be time given and rhythms created where we withdraw from the crowd, find a desolate place, and do nothing but pray.

See what great love the Father has lavished
on us, that we should be called children of
God! And that is what we are! 1 JOHN 3:1 NIV

GOD LOVES YOU. WE hear it so much that it might've
lost its meaning. The awe of it doesn't land like it used
to. Everybody and their mama uses the word to explain
themselves and how they feel about anything. "I love this
color." "I love that song." "I love this book." Maybe because
it's used by so many humans, when God says it, we think
He means it in the same way. But He doesn't and never will.

God's love is a transcendent, holy, unimaginable love. And
the only reason we have a concept of it at all is because God
exists. "Love comes from God" and "God is love" (1 John
4:7–8 NIV). The first time it shows up in Scripture is when
God tests Abraham and tells him to "take your son, your only
son Isaac, whom you love" (Gen. 22:2). Which, of course,
is the foreshadow of Jesus's words to Nicodemus, "For God
so loved the world, that he gave his only Son, that whoever
believes in him should not perish but have eternal life"
(John 3:16).

One evidence of God's love that supersedes any love we've ever known is that God's love is more than words. Words are easy really. A collection of letters we ascribe meaning to and throw them around like confetti. We say things we don't mean and mean things we say. But with God, His Word always corresponds to His intentions and nature "so shall my word be that goes out from my mouth; it shall not return to me empty, but it shall accomplish that which I purpose, and shall succeed in the thing for which I sent it" (Isa. 55:11). God loved us in word and deed and proved it by sacrificing the One He's always loved. "God shows his love for us in that while we were still sinners, Christ died for us" (Rom. 5:8).

Think about it again, that word *sinners*. That collection of people, born opposing God's love and law. Light and life. No sinner deserves God's love in the way He's proved it, but we've received it anyway. A grace, yes. His love too.

Even now, you might be thinking but unwilling to say it out loud, how you know all of this already. The love that motivated the sacrifice of the Son for sinners. But even if you do know about God's love, how deep do you know it? Do you know that it surpasses knowledge? That you need strength to comprehend it? That there is a height, depth, breadth, and length to God's love that, in communion with all of the saints, will fill you with all the fullness of God (Eph. 3:18–20)? There is a difference between knowing about the love of God and *knowing* the love of God. And the good news is, whether you know it or not, God loves you anyway.

For who is God, but the LORD?
And who is a rock, except our God? PSALM 18:31

EVERY DAY WE AWAKE to worship. The one worshipped isn't always the same though. Sometimes we build an altar and offer sacrifices to a different god from the One who made heaven and earth. Sometimes it's a job; other times it's a person. Sometimes it's a worldview that the apostles wouldn't affirm. Other times it's a lie we're addicted to believing.

The true God, Creator of everything that is made, is merciful still. He knows that everything besides Him is but sand. It moves, changes. Is fluid like oceans. Mutable like our selves. Which is to say, none of it is secure. Not the job, the family, the fame, the status, the body—none of it is as solid as it seems. This is why we can't build on it and expect anything more than instability. "Everyone who hears these words of mine and does not do them will be like a foolish man who built his house on the sand. And the rain fell, and the floods came, and the winds blew and beat against that house, and it fell, and great was the fall of it" (Matt. 7:26–27). This is the part where we should pause and consider the mercy of suffering. Trials are like the heavy hand of God, shaking our little kingdoms without our permission. The suffering sifts and sanctifies by exposing the insufficiency of the created things that have our trust and, at the same time, revealing where unbelief exists. As it happens, the foundation beneath us shifts. It's disorienting to discover that the ground underneath your feet isn't strong enough to hold you. Your problems—more than that, your sins—are too heavy for a worldly thing to handle.

Please know this is good news. The destruction of a false kingdom is the grace of God at work. How do I know? Because when it all falls down, when all the thrones you've built your life around shape-shift into the sand they've always been, guess who will still be standing? The King of glory. The unchanging, unwavering, always faithful God. For what other reason do the psalmists constantly call Him "a rock," a "strong tower," and a "refuge"? It is because in Him and in Him alone is eternal stability. In Him, you come to a kingdom that cannot be shaken. When the rain comes and the winds blow, the house stood. This is why the hymnist wrote:

> *My hope is built on nothing less.*
> *Than Jesus' blood and righteousness;*
> *I dare not trust the sweetest frame,*
> *But wholly lean on Jesus' name.*
>
> *On Christ, the solid rock, I stand:*
> *All other ground is sinking sand;*
> *All other ground is sinking sand.*[12]

When the morning comes, sing it aloud. When the evening arrives, do it again. Remember the rock. Only in Christ will you not be moved.

NOTES

1. C. S. Lewis, "Reflections: Half-Hearted Creatures," C. S. Lewis Institute, November 2008, https://www.cslewisinstitute.org/resources/reflections-november-2008.

2. Rich Villodas, *Deeply Formed Life: Five Transformative Values to Root Us in the Way of Jesus* (Colorado Springs: WaterBrook: 2021), 59.

3. Eli Wiesel, *Night* (New York: Hill and Wang, 2006), 68.

4. C. S. Lewis, *The Weight of Glory* (San Francisco: HarperOne, 2001), 46.

5. Hannah Anderson, *All That's Good: Recovering the Lost Art of Discernment* (Chicago, IL: Moody Publishers, 2018), 128.

6. *KJV Spurgeon Study Bible* (Nashville: Holman Bible, 2018), 25.

7. J. R. Edwards, *The Gospel According to Mark* (Grand Rapids: Eerdmans, 2002).

8. Tim Keller, *Every Good Endeavor: Connecting Your Work to God's Work* (New York: Penguin Books, 2014), 338.

9. Anne Trafton, "An Unforgettable Life," MIT News, May 14, 2013, https://news.mit.edu/2013/suzanne-corkin-permanent-present-tense-0514.

10. Dan Allender and Tremper Longman, *The Cry of the Soul: How Our Emotions Reveal Our Deepest Questions about God* (Colorado Springs: NavPress, 2015), 167.

11. Rich Villodas, *Deeply Formed Life*, 45.

12. Edward Mote, "My Hope Is Built on Nothing Less," public domain, accessed February 20, 2023, https://hymnary.org/text/my_hope_is_built_on_nothing_less.

KEEP YOURSELVES IN THE
LOVE OF GOD.

Jude 1:21a

In this 7-session study from Jackie Hill Perry,
dive into themes of being called, loved, and kept,
and learn how to point others to Jesus in grace
and truth. We serve others well when we share
the whole gospel with them, not just the parts
deemed attractive by our culture.

Available where books are sold